Reordering Ranganathan:

Shifting User Behaviors, Shifting Priorities

Lynn Silipigni Connaway, Ph.D.
Senior Research Scientist, OCLC Research

Ixchel M. Faniel, Ph.D.
Associate Research Scientist, OCLC Research

OCLC Research

Reordering Ranganathan: Shifting User Behaviors, Shifting Priorities
Lynn Silipigni Connaway, Ph.D. and Ixchel M. Faniel, Ph.D.

June 2014

OCLC Research
Dublin, Ohio 43017 USA
www.oclc.org

ISBN Print: 1-55653-473-6
                   978-1-55653-473-7

OCLC (WorldCat) #881184214

Please direct correspondence to:
Lynn Silipigni Connaway
Senior Research Scientist
OCLC Research
lynn_connaway@oclc.org

Suggested citation:
Connaway, Lynn Silipigni, and Ixchel M. Faniel. 2014. *Reordering Ranganathan: Shifting User Behaviors,
Shifting Priorities*. Dublin, OH: OCLC Research.
http://www.oclc.org/content/dam/research/publications/library/2014/oclcresearch-reordering-ranganathan-2014.pdf.

ACKNOWLEDGMENTS

We would like to thank those who worked with us on this project. Without the help of Andy Havens, Brad Gauder and Tom Storey for their insightful contributions and valuable feedback; Julianna Barrera-Gomez, Alyssa Darden, Erin M. Hood and Carrie Vass for their dedicated research support; Tam Dalrymple, Larry Olszewski and Jennifer Smither for their thoughtful comments; and Renee Page for her talented design and layout expertise, it would have been difficult to make this report a reality.

Some of the data and material included in this report was from the following projects with support from several funding agencies and institutions.

- *A Cyberinfrastructure Evaluation of the George E. Brown, Jr. Network for Earthquake Engineering Simulation (NEES)*, which was funded by the National Science Foundation (CMMI-0714116).

- *The Cyber Synergy: Seeking Sustainability through Collaboration between Virtual Reference and Social Q&A Sites*, which was funded by the Institution of Museum and Library Services (LG-06-11-0342-11) in collaboration with OCLC Research, and Rutgers, The State University of New Jersey.

- The *Digital Information Seeker Report,* which was jointly sponsored by Jisc and OCLC Research.

- The *Digital Visitors and Residents: What Motivates Engagement with the Digital Information Environment?* project, which was funded by Jisc in collaboration with the University of Oxford, OCLC Research, and the University of North Carolina.

- The *Dissemination Information Packages for Information Reuse (DIPIR)* project, which was funded by the Institute for Museum and Library Services (LG-06-10-0140-10) in collaboration with the University of Michigan.

- The *Seeking Synchronicity: Evaluating Virtual Reference Services from User, Non-user and Librarian Perspectives*, which was funded by the Institution of Museum and Library Services (LG-06-05-0109-05) in collaboration with OCLC Research, and Rutgers, The State University of New Jersey.

- The *Virtual Research Environment (VRE) Study*, which was a collaborative project between Jisc and OCLC Research.

Lynn Silipigni Connaway
Senior Research Scientist
OCLC Research

Ixchel M. Faniel
Associate Research Scientist
OCLC Research

i

TABLE OF CONTENTS

Same Laws,
New Lens.

Reordering Ranganathan

Introduction

1	Books are for use.
2	Every person his or her book.
3	Every book its reader.
4	Save the time of the reader.
5	A library is a growing organism.

—Ranganathan 1931

In 1931, Shiyali Ramamrita Ranganathan, a mathematician and librarian who is widely regarded as a founder of modern library science, proposed his *Five Laws of Library Science* (Ranganathan 1931). His five laws have provided powerful guidance for generations of librarians. As a framework for evaluating library programs, policies and strategies, there is probably not a single document as widely known, respected and referenced even today, more than 80 years after its publication.

In fact, what we've seen are numerous efforts to apply the five laws to more recent trends in information services, most specifically electronic materials and the Web. Changing or adding to the laws to incorporate other forms of media isn't that much of a stretch. Ranganathan and his contemporaries, even in the 1930s, probably would have considered these changes to be part of his original doctrine. After all, there were magazines, newspapers, film and audio recordings in the 30s. Microfiche had come into commercial use the decade before, and in 1924 the Computing-Tabulating-Recording Company changed its name to the International Business Machines Corporation—IBM—after having revolutionized the storage of data on punch cards.

In short, there is no reason to suppose that Ranganathan didn't mean for books to be a stand-in for any and all media that a library might now, or ever, collect, catalog and circulate. The idea that we would one day encode information in digital format and share it using worldwide, interconnected computers probably would not have caused Ranganathan to change his language. "Books are for use" is simply too powerful a statement and too succinct to warrant much improvement.

The other major event in the history of librarianship from 1931 was the death of Melvil Dewey. Ranganathan had corresponded with Dewey briefly and had sent him an early copy of the *Five Laws*, and he was gratified to receive a reply from a man he thought of as an inspiration. During a speech in 1964, Ranganathan credited his decision to become a librarian to his first discovery of the Dewey Decimal Classification ® (DDC) system. And he was deeply saddened that Dewey had passed away before they had a chance to truly collaborate.

In the time of Dewey and Ranganathan, the first law, "books are for use," was the driver. Both men came from backgrounds in which information scarcity was the rule of the day, and the desire to protect library collections was a much greater professional concern to librarians than it is now. Closed stacks were the rule in Dewey's time, and chaining books to shelves was not uncommon. In a world where publishing was still relatively expensive and copies of important books might be incredibly rare, librarians were gatekeepers more often than greeters or information guides. Dewey specifically developed the DDC to address this issue, inventing a system that is both understandable by the public and not tied to any specific library or librarian's methods. A classification system is, essentially, a way for anyone anywhere to understand how to access materials.

In short, "books are for use."

Books still hold a powerful place in our cultural psyche. Whether a book is read on leather-bound thick sheets of paper or a smartphone screen, the point isn't (and probably never has been) the medium. When we say, "I just read a great book," we don't mean the action of sitting down, licking a thumb, turning the page and moving our eyes over the words. Those actions are the same for every person who ever read a book, and they're not particularly interesting.

What we mean, of course, is that we enjoyed spending time transferring someone else's thoughts into our own. We had a positive experience digesting new information. Our effort was worthwhile. Conversely, when we say, "Oh, it was an awful book," we don't mean that the pages were yellow or that it smelled funny. We mean it was not worth our time.

These same experiences hold true for information or entertainment in any media. A Facebook like or Tweet about a research presentation or a review on Goodreads transmits the same message: "I [processed] this [content], and I would [recommend / not recommend] it to [audience]." These and the following examples are all, essentially, new ways of saying, "books are for use," "every person his or her book," or "every book its reader":

- Facebook post for a YouTube video;

- Embedded link to a scholarly article in a blog post;

- Good Google search rank on a particular phrase;

- Book cover picture on a Pinterest page.

The difference is that they are for very large, complex and increasingly creative values of reader and book. Applying Ranganathan's laws to the current environment shows, in fairly stark terms, the difference between the time in which Dewey and Ranganathan worked and the information environment in which we operate today (Table I1). We have moved from an era of content scarcity to one of incredible abundance and diversity, which is being contributed to by a multitude of channels and contributors. These differences are at the center of what has changed the interpretations of the five laws.

Table I1. Ranganathan's five laws: Original vs. new conceptions

	Ranganathan's Original Conception	New Conceptions in the Current Environment		
First Law	Books are for use.	E-books are for reading.	Netflix is for watching.	Blackboard is for studying.
Second Law	Every person his or her book.	Every listener her iTunes.	Every artist his Photoshop.	Every student her EasyBib.
Third Law	Every book its reader.	Every blog its reader.	Every Google Map, its traveler.	Every digital repository its researcher.
Fourth Law	Save the time of the reader.	Save the time of the listener.	Save the time of the traveler.	Save the time of the researcher.
Fifth Law	A library is a growing organism.			

Interestingly the fifth law—"a library is a growing organism"—has not changed from its original conception. In fact, sometime over the last two decades, it went from an important observation to a cliché. Of course the library is growing. How can it not grow when the information environment has expanded so incredibly for everyone, not just libraries? Under the circumstances, it would have taken a tremendous effort *not* to grow.

It used to be that books were guarded by librarians who employed unique, local methods for storing and retrieving materials. Now we have an increasingly daunting array of content facilitated by librarians for individuals to discover, access and share. From libraries that store books and librarians who help find local, physical content, we now have a world in which libraries must provide access to not only externally produced content but also content produced within the academic community (Dempsey 2012). Librarians must move beyond their doors and out into the world in order to bring the world's content back to the community and to make the content created in the academic community available to the world. Whether considering outreach programs, in-class instruction, collections, research teams or virtual reference services, what we find is an increasing move to expand the places in which librarianship occurs and the tools librarians use to help those they serve achieve their goals.

But if materials have become so abundant that "books are for use" is now less about scarcity and more about choice, availability, find-ability and share-ability, what does that do to the five laws?

We are not suggesting that it is time to abandon the laws, not by any stretch. They are still an enormously helpful way to link the values of librarianship with concrete programs and activities.

In a world where information is becoming increasingly abundant in multiple formats and in a variety of settings, we suggest a reordering of the five laws. This will help us keep topmost in our mind the way in which the digital and Web revolutions have transformed the balance in our relationships with the academic community, resources and services.

In the next five chapters, we'll look at what today's librarians, library researchers and information scientists have said about the changing roles of the five laws and examples of how the laws are put in practice today. We also will review relevant literature that helps, in aggregate, show how the five laws still apply, but where, we believe, it's time for a change in focus and emphasis. Findings from our research on user behavior also will be included to show how the *Five Laws of Library Science* is as relevant today as it was in 1931. Each chapter will include a bibliography, so readers can continue their research of the topic beyond the scope of this brief overview.

In an increasingly abundant information environment, the laws of nature may not have changed, even though nature itself has. In other words, Ranganathan's five laws still apply in today's radically different information environment. If there is scarcity among patrons today, it is of something else that Ranganathan addresses in the five laws: time. In our retelling, we promote "save the time of the reader" to number one on the list; the one law that should guide the interpretation and application of the other four.

References

Dempsey, Lorcan. 2012. Thirteen ways of looking at libraries, discovery, and the catalog: Scale, workflow, attention. *EDUCAUSE Review Online* (December 10, 2012), http://www.educause.edu/ero/article/thirteen-ways-looking-libraries-discovery-and-catalog-scale-workflow-attention.

Ranganathan, Shiyali Ramamrita. 1931. *The five laws of library science*. London: Edward Goldston, Ltd.

1

Save the time
of the reader.

> " Perhaps this law is not so self-evident as the others. None the less, it has been responsible for many reforms in library administration and has a great potential for effecting many more reforms in the future. Perhaps the most convenient method of studying the consequences of this law will be to follow the reader from the moment he enters the library to the moment he leaves it, critically examining each process, which he has to go through, with an eye to the economy of time that can be effected at each stage."
> **—Ranganathan 1931, 337**

The new first law: Save the time of the reader

As Ranganathan predicted, the fourth law, "save the time of the reader," has risen in importance as the requirements for the first three laws have been progressively satisfied. Given the vast array of content being offered through a multitude of information service providers, scarcity of time and attention is one of the most pressing issues facing people today. Consequently, we believe "save the time of the reader" has become the most important of Ranganathan's five laws and should be the lens through which we interpret a useful reading of the others.

In order to improve the user's experience in the physical library, Ranganathan believed it was necessary to minimize the amount of time it took to get what the user wanted. Hence, the new first law "save the time of the reader." Although saving time is still very important, research suggests that convenience also has become important to today's information seekers (Connaway, Dickey, and Radford 2011; Connaway, Lanclos, and Hood 2013b). As libraries have begun to operate alongside other information service providers, such as Google, Amazon and Facebook, how people experience library services, particularly online service, has become more important (Dempsey 2012). These three aspects of time are discussed in this chapter:

- Time as simply time; a measure of minutes; how long it takes a user to achieve a desired outcome

- Time as a shorthand for convenience or almost any efficiency-based value that users ascribe to their experience with a library

- Time as stand-in for the entire service experience beyond the actual quality of content, materials, resources, etc.

Examining the law in today's environment

"Save the time of the reader," although succinctly stated, touches many aspects of how the library designs, develops and delivers its services; and if applied correctly, the results have the potential to be transformative (Gorman 1998, 21). Preserving, cataloging, presenting and distributing content are still important aspects of librarianship. However, how these activities are done and how services are provided and made available has become increasingly important. Patrons want to satisfy their information needs not only quickly, but also conveniently. Consequently, libraries must deliver online services that are compelling enough to attract their intended community (Glassmeyer 2010; Goldup 2010; Kwanya, Stilwell, and Underwood 2010).

> Provide metasearching capabilities so that users can search entire sets of electronic resources. And link resolvers so that readers get access to the best source."
> **—Cloonan and Dove 2005, 59**

> A webmaster should think about users and how to attract them, develop for them, cater to them, if s/he wants to satisfy the Web community."
> **—Noruzi 2004**

Time as time

"Time as time" is the most literal reading of the law, and we see its importance in ongoing research. Its significance can be linked to rational choice theory. It's also supported by Savolainen's (1993) concept of time as a context in information seeking and gratification, which emphasizes time constraints that are based on an individual's situation. What's different today is that it operates within the bounds of different resources and information activities. Today, people are inundated with information that they have to review and evaluate to make choices, and time has become a significant constraint as a result (Connaway, Dickey, and Radford 2011). They also are contributing more information. Moreover, many information activities are taking place online.

Recently, a graduate student writing instructor described how his students' information searches for their research projects had evolved from browsing books in the stacks to submitting online queries to Google, in part because it is quicker (Alves 2013). "Millennials, by their own admission, have no tolerance for delays" (Sweeney 2006, 3). They respond quickly to communications from others and expect the same in return (Oblinger and Oblinger 2005), especially from their information sources (Connaway 2008; Connaway and Radford 2007; Connaway and Radford 2011; Connaway, Radford, Dickey, Williams, and Confer 2008; Van Scoyoc and Cason 2006). According to a 2012 Pew Research Center report, teachers report time management as an issue among their students, finding that digital technologies "encourage students to assume all tasks can be finished quickly and at the last minute" (Purcell et al. 2012).

Yet, librarians and instructors still are adjusting to meet the needs of students given this shift. Undergraduate and graduate students reported a preference for searching the Web instead of the online library catalog, because the Web was fast and easy (Fast and Campbell 2004). Not surprisingly, the Internet and Wikipedia are used extensively to get an initial overview of a topic (Prabha, Connaway, and Dickey 2006). Head and Eisenberg report that "almost all" of the students in their study "used course readings, library resources, and public Internet sites such as Google and Wikipedia, when conducting course-related research" (2009, 32). However, students' use of Wikipedia has been compared to a "covert, underground Learning Black Market" (Connaway, Lanclos, and Hood 2013a, 2013b, 293; White 2011). Although used extensively, its use often is not acknowledged. In the United States and the United Kingdom, students reported citing references in Wikipedia articles, but not the actual Wikipedia articles, because they believed instructors did not value them as much as traditional information sources (Connaway, Lanclos, and Hood 2013a, 2013b; Connaway, Lanclos et al. 2013; Connaway, White et al. 2013). In a recent essay, one instructor clarified his position, noting the benefits of online information sources but also contending, "Part of our mission as teachers is to counteract the preferences that students bring with them and to help them adopt those that enable them not just to gather and scan information efficiently, but also to pursue their interests more purposefully—to encourage them to think and write more deeply, more reflectively, and more creatively" (Alves 2013).

> " Last semester I was writing a paper on Brazil and there was a book in the library that I just did not want to leave my house to go to. It is a 50-minute drive, I didn't want to do that, but I was writing my paper and so I used Google books instead and really they only had a section of the book available but that was the section I used. So, you know, doing that instead of coming here physically and going to get the whole book. And it saved time, it saved gas, I got what I needed and it wasn't a big deal."
> —US Graduate Student #4, Female, Age 23, Latin American Studies, Digital Visitors and Residents

Librarians also have been adjusting their systems and services for scholars who are now required to provide better management and more accurate metadata for their scholarly work, including research data. Operating within time constraints is an issue under these circumstances as well, especially in the absence of automated methods for metadata generation (Connaway and Dickey 2010b). Earthquake engineering researchers were found to delay contributing data to a central repository because uploading and documenting the data were time- and labor-intensive processes without the benefit of automated tools and guidelines to support how they worked (Faniel 2009).

Research suggests more communication and collaboration are needed between the developers and users of information systems and services (Connaway and Dickey 2010b; Faniel 2009). It is critical to understand and support how scholars work in the midst of improving their efficiency. As one digital repository manager observed, systems helped scholars "work faster, but not necessarily better" (Connaway and Dickey 2010b, 3). This may be one reason for the limited uptake of the systems, services and guidelines that are available. For instance, national and professional bodies in archeology have developed guidelines for data documentation to describe the types of documentation expected, preferred file formats and data points desired (e.g., Aitchinson 2009; Brown 2007; Brown and Perrin 2000; Institute for Archaeologists 2009; Parks Canada 2005). However, the guidelines often do not accommodate the realities of field research, so their use in the area has been limited (Faniel et al. 2013).

> "
>
> I think one thing is just finding the time. When we create large enough data it just seems like an extra effort to actually upload the information. I think going along with that in order to document what that file is or what that information is also requires a lot of effort on our part in order to really make it understandable for the next person to look at the information … So creating the metadata for each file is part of the extra effort."
> — **Graduate Student, NEES User #14, A Cyberinfrastructure Evaluation of NEES**

Time as convenience

People often mention convenience in the same breath as efficiency, but it encompasses more than the number of minutes it takes to fulfill an information need. Research suggests convenience is more important to people than quick service (Connaway, Dickey, and Radford 2011; Connaway, Lanclos, and Hood 2013b). Convenience is defined as "(1) fitness or suitability for performing an action or fulfilling a requirement; and (2) something (as an appliance, device, service) conducive to comfort or ease" (Merriam-Webster.com). Convenience can be physical or virtual and is based on the context and situation at the time of the need (Connaway 2013a, 2013b; Connaway, Lanclos et al. 2013; Connaway, White et al. 2013). Context provides the background within which individuals understand and explain (Talja, Keso, and Pietilainen 1999). Situation, a narrower concept, refers to the time and space where sense is constructed (Case 2012; Savolainen 1993). For instance, campus information commons, with 24/7 access to materials, facilities and cafes, are popular because they are convenient for individuals who operate outside of the traditional bounds of a 9-to-5 workday (Connaway 2013a).

Convenience plays a role in people's choices and actions throughout the information-seeking process. It influences people's choice of and satisfaction with physical and electronic sources as well as their perceptions about ease of use and personal time horizons (Connaway, Dickey, and Radford 2011). So what does the research say about the convenience of libraries? Some people are frustrated with libraries and avoid in-person visits because of limited hours, long travel distances and the time needed to do their research in the library (Connaway 2013b; Connaway, Lanclos, and Hood 2013b; Connaway, Lanclos et al. 2013; Pullinger 1999). Search engines are preferred not only because they are faster but also because they are more convenient—easier to use, cost-effective and reliable (i.e., always available) (De Rosa 2005). A set of resources may be used consistently simply because that method is now predictable and familiar (Head and Eisenberg 2009). A study reported that 74% of respondents did not choose the Internet because it was the best source; they chose the Internet because it was the most convenient or easiest to use (93%) and did not cost much in time or money (69%) (Griffiths and King 2008). The Internet is a convenient way to get information at or through a library (Idaho Commission for Libraries 2007). Similarly, virtual reference services (VRS) are used primarily for convenience (Connaway and Radford 2011).

> "
> It's really cool that nowadays you don't have to go to the library to find a book, it's right there on your laptop...it beats wasting gas to go to the library just to get a book when you can find it online with no trouble."
> —US Graduate Student #4, Female, Age 23, Latin American Studies, Digital Visitors and Residents

In a study of Millennial undergraduate students, convenience and speed made Google their first choice, followed by human sources, such as parents and friends (Connaway et al. 2008). When Millennials did use library sources, they tended to use electronic sources and often were unaware that they came from the library (Connaway, Lanclos, and Hood 2013b). Millennials also associated the authority of information sources with convenience, particularly sources their tutors, teachers and library staff identified, including syllabus-based websites (Connaway, White et al. 2013). These sources were convenient because they were recommended by trusted third parties and were integrated into the students' workflows. Convenient information selection also was based on Millennials weighing the cost of their time against the benefits of their potential grade on assignments (Connaway 2008, 2013b; Connaway and Radford 2007, 2011; Connaway, Lanclos, and Hood 2013b; Connaway, Lanclos et al. 2013; Connaway et al. 2008). Information searches were curtailed as a result. The undergraduates only did the minimum search necessary to meet their assignment requirements. In other words, they satisficed. Satisfice is a combination of the words satisfy and suffice. Herb Simon (1957) coined the term to explain how individuals often settle for whatever can be accomplished within specific, predetermined criteria based on the context and situation of the need. In other words, individuals often settle for "good enough" instead of pursuing the optimal solution if convenience outweighs the benefit.

> ❝ What I'll do is I'll just Google it. And it's like 'Oh, I need this. Hold on.' And I was like 'Specifically it involves these three words—bam, bam, bam.' And then whatever comes up. And if I'm not satisfied with that I'll try another set of words until I get it. And then it depends on the time. So let's say like I only had five minutes, I would probably do it three times and if I haven't found it by the third time I'm going to settle with whatever is there."
> —US Graduate Student #5, Female, Age 30, Latin American Studies, Digital Visitors and Residents

Time as user experience

While time can be measured in precise increments, in many cases the service experience determines how much can be usefully accomplished within a set timeframe. A century ago, library services were focused on architecture, physical workflow design and urban planning. A long walk between sections of a library or an out-of-reach shelf was essentially a time barrier and an inconvenience. Planning the physical environment is still important, but more often than not, it serves as the backdrop for patrons operating in a world dominated by online information sources. Consequently, libraries also must adhere to best practices in Web design and information flow. Moreover, the experience and preference of library users is being affected by other, nonlibrary services such as Amazon, Google, Facebook, Twitter, and social question and answer sites, etc., all of which have set a high bar for how people experience the Web. We see evidence of the shift in the current literature, particularly the expectations people have about their online service experience.

Library catalogs have long been the point of discovery and delivery of content. However, today's patrons are more likely to find out about material using other online sources. Web searching has driven higher expectations for online library catalogs. People want to find information quickly and conveniently, and they expect the interface to be familiar to them, which means seeing their search results rated, reviewed and ranked by relevancy (Calhoun et al. 2009; Connaway 2013b; Connaway, Dickey, and Radford 2011; Connaway, Lanclos, and Hood 2013b; Connaway, Lanclos et al. 2013; Connaway and Radford 2011; Connaway, White et al. 2013; Dempsey 2012). With unfamiliar resources, or just too many, students can be frustrated by the overwhelming amount of information available (Head and Eisenberg 2009; Purcell et al. 2012).

> ❝ But now it just seems like…online you have more access. You don't have to come here. You don't have to call. It just seems like it's easier to find something in researching."
> —US Graduate Student #3, Female, Age 23, History, Digital Visitors and Residents

Unfortunately, libraries have not consistently employed their usage data to fully mobilize discovery services in the same way as Google (Dempsey 2012). This is why some people use Amazon.com to discover resources before going to the online library catalog to search its availability and location (Connaway et al. 2008). Providing seamless points of access to the content people discover through other online services could be a point of distinction for libraries. A focus group study reported that people ranked delivery of their items as "important, if not more important, than his or her discovery experience" (Calhoun et al. 2009, v). Another study concluded that access—not discovery—is the major challenge for today's information seekers, who may be better served by online library catalogs that improve delivery and provide more links to more online content (Connaway and Dickey 2010a).

> **"** I will want some like intelligent device to filter everything for me...so I can save my time from, you know, wasting it on filtering everything by myself."
> —**UK Graduate Student #1, Female, Age 23, Learning and Technology, Digital Visitors and Residents**

Still, in the age of seemingly limitless online content, librarians will need to balance access against users' needs and time demands (Connaway et al. 2008). It is true that services like Google help people discover content more quickly and conveniently, but their search results often leave them wanting more. When faced with sifting through a lot of content, people want search engines that return information relevant to their search queries in order to minimize their need to evaluate the content (White et al. 2012).

It's important not only to provide users the means to discover and access content but also to contribute and share content. Consequently, some libraries provide research data services that include virtual research environments and/or institutional repositories. In these instances librarians' awareness of user needs from the perspective of those contributing and accessing the content is paramount to providing systems and services that will be valued and adopted. Earthquake engineering researchers resisted using many of the systems and services provided in a virtual research environment designed to facilitate collaboration and data sharing, because they were not intuitive or seen as offering much advantage over existing tools, such as telephone and e-mail (Faniel 2009). Developed with little input from the researchers, the resulting systems and services were not easy to use and alienated the researchers rather than engaged them.

> "
> Getting data into the repository is not hard. Getting anything back out is hard for me as the owner of that data and at this stage I would say next to impossible for a conventional user...if I look at a diagram for my test specimen and there's a certain instrument that I'm interested in looking at what the data was, it takes me several steps to go from that diagram to the data. Lots of clicks in other words. Now I'm beginning to get a feel for the system so I sort of know what the clicks are but a regular user wouldn't know that and there's very little guidance."
> **—Professor, NEES User #4, A Cyberinfrastructure Evaluation of NEES**

Time—whether a precise measurement, a stand-in for convenience or one aspect of user experience—is the resource that people need help managing more than any other. If librarians choose to address time by simply keeping pace with changing tools and technologies, they are missing the point. Static websites became online library catalogs and Flickr pages became Pinterests. Librarians have to acknowledge that individuals have relocated much of their information activities to the Internet; therefore, librarians need to utilize the Web as a place to engage people in new and different ways. Understanding the offline and online lives of our communities will reveal opportunities to engage with them at times and in ways that are both natural and surprising.

Our interpretation of the law

Libraries represent a very small subset of the information resources and activities people need today. As we said earlier, laws may not change, but sometimes nature itself does. And the new environment our users find themselves in challenges librarians to move from a simple declaration of "save the time of the reader" to a more complex and interconnected priority of:

Embed library systems and services into users' existing workflows.

People don't have the time to use systems and services that don't fit into the way they work, especially if they can find other ways to accomplish their goals. The library and its catalog and services did not have much competition prior to the widespread use of the Internet, but now there is a need to be integrated at the network level in order to be a visible and viable part of users' workflows (Dempsey 2008).

While critical, embedding library systems and services into users' existing workflows can be difficult. It requires being attuned to users' lives, work and needs (Faniel 2009) and educating them about the potential to streamline some of their work processes (Connaway and Dickey 2010b). It also requires that librarians look outside of their own library-controlled environments.

Even if forced to visit libraries because of the requirements of specific content, people will be less than satisfied and less likely to support future library efforts. People are now comparing the time (minutes, convenience, user experience) taken to discover, access and/or contribute content at a library with other media and information services and choosing to go elsewhere.

A library should not add procedural drag to the information activities of its community. We can't ask our users to learn separate systems for accessing separate types of media. We can't ask scholars to learn one more metadata scheme in order to make their research appear in different collections. We can't ask students to click through page after page of links trying to find the database with the article they need.

To address the imperative of this law, the library needs to move from an institutional resource to a network resource. We need to provide better, more natural links to library resources in places like Wikipedia and other network services. In that way, people will be able to discover, access and contribute content through other channels besides the library. Dempsey (2012) refers to this as the "inside-out" case.

People make decisions every day on their preferred methods of searching for information. Our best bet to save their time—and, thus, ensure that they are satisfied, if not delighted, with our services—is to embed what we do in what they do, rather than asking the reverse.

How can librarians make that happen? Start by accepting "save the time of the reader" as the first law, then modify approaches to the other laws accordingly. We address the latter in the next few chapters.

Before we proceed, here are some ways for librarians to start rethinking how to apply the spirit of the "save the time of the reader" law.

Recommendations

While our interpretation of "save the time of the reader" will color our review of the other laws, we recommend an initial set of guidelines for thinking about the use of this law as it applies to service assessment, evaluation and development.

Inform

Our first suggestion is to inform users. Our recommendations for doing so draw from the findings of the Digital Visitors and Residents project that examines what motivates individuals' engagement with the digital information environment (Connaway, Lanclos, and Hood 2013b). Specifically, we recommend that librarians reexamine their systems and services in the context of how they do the following:

- Market and promote library services;

- Provide a broad range of tools;

- Remove the barriers between discovering and accessing information.

It goes without saying that most commercial information services have a much bigger marketing and promotion budget than most libraries. The goal here, though, isn't to directly advertise library services as competitors of those already in use. It is to make the total package of library services appealing as part of a much larger discussion and set of behaviors. It is also to make the results gained from using the library so transformative and inspiring that they stand out as unique and essential elements of the modern information ecosystem.

This is an education issue for librarians as much as it is for library users. Our recommendation to provide a broad range of tools means that we need to investigate what users are actually doing and the technologies they are employing. It's not enough to put readers' advisory posts on a blog. Are they also available as an e-mail update? On Pinterest? On Facebook? Tumblr? Twitter? It may feel like redundant work, but remember that the intention is to remove barriers. And one of these barriers is that librarians often try to change users' preferences rather than service as many user preferences as reasonably possible.

Individuals will be inspired when the high-quality, authoritative and unique materials and services librarians have spent time collecting and making available are easily found in a variety of workflows. They will experience "A-ha!" moments without expressly asking for help. That final result—exposure to surprising and unique materials within current workflows—means that the time spent was worth it. And if the library is involved in that process, then the library is seen as saving the time of the user and being part of that success.

Be seamless

Consider walking through the library's workflow from the perspective of a user trying to accomplish a particular task. How often do you leave one interface and go to another? Every time that happens, individuals have to reevaluate their surroundings, which often equates to a direct loss of time or, at least, a poorly perceived experience.

How often do u-turns or dead-ends in a process not provide any way to proceed, other than going back to the beginning? Seamlessness is not just about doing something efficiently. It often will require that librarians spend as much or more time working with external systems as internal systems. This should be viewed not as an inconvenient distraction but as a requirement. Rather than acting as a librarian with an intimate knowledge of internal systems and services, role-play a specific person who is familiar with only a single search box in a Web browser. Are you deeply satisfied with the resource provided? How do you get there without having to navigate more sophisticated library systems? Thinking of the people who use library systems should be an integral part of the design and functionality of these systems in order to provide seamless access to resources (Connaway and Dickey 2010a).

Be proactive

Being proactive is about more than just promotion. A study of a virtual research environment concluded that support staff needed to better anticipate the challenges it would encounter as the user community's needs continued to grow and change (Faniel 2009). Drawing from the study, this approach requires librarians to be proactive providers of systems and services rather than reactive ones who wait for challenges to arise. Instead of waiting to follow prescribed plans (which may or may not come to fruition), librarians must sense and respond to challenges across user communities. This requires paying close attention to what currently is going on inside and outside of the library environment to determine what might happen next.

Be bold, be inventive and take risks. Librarians can't wait for other people or groups within the organization to propose a solution that would help save users' time. This is not to suggest that cooperation is not important. In fact, being proactive may mean actively seeking out important partnerships. But it also means that if users' pain points are understood, librarians shouldn't wait for someone else to address them.

How do librarians go about understanding those pain points? Listen. Watch. Ask people how they accomplish tasks now. Ask what frustrates them. In many cases, the answer most definitely will not be found within the library. But if enough evidence and knowledge about those areas that need the most work is accumulated, paths to success will become clear.

Look upstream

Looking upstream is about more than proactively considering user communities' current needs. It's seeing those needs in a much larger context and thinking broadly within the information profession and other professions related to it. There are a number of factors that might be influencing people's choices about the systems and services they use. Consider the development and delivery of research data services. Knowledge of funding agency mandates, the existence of disciplinary data repositories, supportive tools and researchers' need for and confidence in their data management skills can help librarians better shape and advertise the library's capabilities, systems and services in response (Faniel and Zimmerman 2011). Similarly, how are changes in academia affecting not just our scholars and students but also alumni and parents? How are changes in journalism changing our expectations of bias? How are legal issues related to intellectual property affecting our ability to keep and expose content? What about privacy concerns?

People are not making their choices about how to satisfy their information needs in a vacuum. Researchers do not wake up one morning and decide, "I'm going to stop reading so many paper journals and start spending some of that time watching YouTube videos of live conference presentations." Students do not decide, "This is the year that I'll begin using a citation generator for my bibliographies." They make these decisions in an increasingly complex and rich environment. They may make a new choice because of a need to decrease spending. They may have access to a new device like an iPad or smartphone. They may have a service that they use for home entertainment that, lo-and-behold, also is useful at work. More likely than not, the service will be linked to or recommended by a friend or colleague.

And since being involved in the wider information environment requires being open to partnerships, looking upstream can help identify early opportunities for cooperation. Are students using a particular social networking service for photos? If so, is there a way to apply that technology to digital objects, reviews, special events, etc.? If users are early adopters of a service, librarians should think about how to meet them there with library resources sooner rather than later.

Conclusion

Which sounds more appealing?

> "I have the answer to the question you just asked…"

> "I have an answer to the question that will be important to you tomorrow…"

> "I know what questions you should be asking…"

Since the beginning of the Industrial Revolution, we have been looking for ways to save time. We all say, "time is money," and we mean it almost literally. In addition, we are a future-focused society. Our search for the most current information (even about the past) is often at the service of forward-looking goals. We want to improve our chances of getting the next job, finding a new cure, developing a successful business. Time is at the center of that calculation, too, as we are constantly thinking not just about what we need to know today but also what we'll need to know to complete the next step.

Libraries, some would say, tend to focus more on the past. "Cultural heritage" or "memory institutions" imply a focus on maintaining the records and materials of our shared history. Within the history of the information profession, the tasks associated with that responsibility have sometimes seemed to favor the service of our materials, the acquisition and preservation of content, rather than that of our communities, the people who always are changing and looking forward. While there is an enormous reserve of community service spirit in the profession, there also is an underlying truth that many librarians are deeply interested in the past, in history, in the preservation of knowledge and in the care of our cultural heritage.

Those two impulses, however—to serve both the materials that define our past and the people who will create our future—are not in opposition. A forward thinker would never claim that we care for the past simply because the past itself is interesting. We do it to help inform and inspire our path into the future.

And that balance point is the place where "save the time of the reader" can be most powerfully applied as a kind of skeleton key to unlock the potential for libraries to brilliantly impact the lives of our communities.

"Save the time of the reader." Why? Because the more opportunities we have to understand our past, our world and ourselves, the more choices we will have in determining our future. Libraries can provide answers. People are moving from a point in their past, defined by a problem, challenge or search, toward a point in the future, defined by the options they have available. Librarians can get involved in that journey and help speed them forward, getting them to where they're going with a faster and more convenient service experience than they thought possible and receiving their enthusiastic, lifelong support in exchange.

References

Aitchison, Kenneth. 2009. Standards and guidance in archaeological archiving: The work of the archaeological archives forum and the institute for archaeologists. *The Grey Journal* 5, no. 2: 67–71. http://www.greynet.org/images/Contents_TGJ.V5.N2.pdf.

Alves, Julio. 2013. Unintentional knowledge: What we find when we're not looking. *The Chronicle of Higher Education: The Chronicle Review* (June 23), http://chronicle.com/article/Unintentional-Knowledge/139891/?cid=cr&utm_source=cr&utm_medium=en.

Brown, Adrian, and Kathy Perrin. 2000. *A model for the description of archaeological archives.* Forth Cumberland: English Heritage Centre for Archaeology. http://www.eng-h.gov.uk/archives/archdesc.pdf.

Brown, Duncan H. 2007. *Archaeological archives: A guide to best practice in creation, compilation, transfer and curation.* n.p.: Archaeological Archives Forum. http://www.archaeologyuk.org/archives/.

Calhoun, Karen, Joanne Cantrell, Peggy Gallagher, and Janet Hawk. 2009. *Online catalogs: What users and librarians want: An OCLC report.* Dublin, OH: OCLC.

Case, Donald Owen. 2012. *Looking for information: A survey of research on information seeking, needs and behavior.* Bingley, UK: Emerald Group.

Cloonan, Michele V., and John G. Dove. 2005. Ranganathan online: Do digital libraries violate the Third Law? *Library Journal* 130, no. 6: 58-60.

Connaway, Lynn Silipigni. 2008. Make room for the Millennials. *NextSpace* 10: 18-19. http://www.oclc.org/nextspace/010/research.htm.

Connaway, Lynn Silipigni. 2013a. Findings from user behavior studies: A user's world. Presented at

ALA Midwinter Meeting and Exhibits, January 28, 2013, in Seattle, WA.

Connaway, Lynn Silipigni. 2013b. Why the internet is more attractive than the library. *The Serials Librarian* 64, no. 1-4: 41-56.

Connaway, Lynn Silipigni, and Timothy J. Dickey. 2010a. *The digital information seeker: Report of findings from selected OCLC, RIN, and JISC user behavior projects*. n.p.: Higher Education Funding Council for England (HEFCE). http://www.jisc.ac.uk/media/documents/publications/reports/2010/digitalinformationseekerreport.pdf.

Connaway, Lynn Silipigni, and Timothy J. Dickey. 2010b. *Towards a profile of the researcher of today: What can we learn from JISC Projects? Common themes identified in an analysis of JISC virtual research environment and digital repository projects*. http://ie-repository.jisc.ac.uk/418/2/VirtualScholar_themesFromProjects_revised.pdf.

Connaway, Lynn Silipigni, Timothy J. Dickey, and Marie L. Radford. 2011. "If it is too inconvenient I'm not going after it:" Convenience as a critical factor in information-seeking behaviors. *Library & Information Science Research* 33, no. 3: 179-90. http://www.oclc.org/content/dam/research/publications/library/2011/connaway-lisr.pdf.

Connaway, Lynn Silipigni, Donna M. Lanclos, and Erin M. Hood. 2013a. "I always stick with the first thing that comes up on Google..." Where people go for information, what they use, and why. *EDUCAUSE Review Online*. http://www.educause.edu/ero/article/i-always-stick-first-thing-comes-google-where-people-go-information-what-they-use-and-why.

Connaway, Lynn Silipigni, Donna Lanclos, and Erin M. Hood. 2013b. "I find Google a lot easier than going to the library website." Imagine ways to innovate and inspire students to use the academic library. *Proceedings of the Association of College & Research Libraries (ACRL) 2013 conference, April 10-13, 2013, Indianapolis, IN*. Chicago: Association of College & Research Libraries. http://www.ala.org/acrl/sites/ala.org.acrl/files/content/conferences/confsandpreconfs/2013/papers/Connaway_Google.pdf.

Connaway, Lynn Silipigni, Donna Lanclos, David White, Alison Le Cornu, and Erin M. Hood. 2013. User-centered decision making: A new model for developing academic library services and systems. *IFLA Journal* 39, no. 1: 30-36.

Connaway, Lynn Silipigni, and Marie L. Radford. 2007. Service sea change: Clicking with screenagers through virtual reference. In *Sailing into the future: Charting our destiny: Proceedings of the Thirteenth National Conference of the Association of College and Research Libraries, March 29-April 1, 2007, Baltimore, Maryland*, edited by Hugh A. Thompson. Chicago: Association of College and Research Libraries. http://www.oclc.org/research/publications/archive/2007/connaway-acrl.pdf.

Connaway, Lynn Silipigni, and Marie L. Radford. 2011. *Seeking synchronicity: Revelations and recommendations for virtual reference*. Dublin, OH: OCLC Research. http://www.oclc.org/reports/synchronicity/full.pdf.

Connaway, Lynn Silipigni, Marie L. Radford, Timothy J. Dickey, Jocelyn De Angelis Williams, and Patrick Confer. 2008. Sense-making and synchronicity: Information-seeking behaviors of Millennials and Baby Boomers. *Libri* 58, no. 2: 123-35. http://www.oclc.org/resources/research/publications/library/2008/connaway-libri.pdf.

Connaway, Lynn Silipigni, David White, Donna Lanclos, and Alison Le Cornu. 2013. Visitors and Residents: What motivates engagement with the digital information environment? *Information Research* 18, no. 1, http://informationr.net/ir/18-1/infres181.html.

Dempsey, Lorcan. 2008. Always on: Libraries in a world of permanent connectivity. *First Monday* 14, no. 1, http://www.firstmonday.org/htbin/cgiwrap/bin/ojs/index.php/fm/article/view/2291/207.

Dempsey, Lorcan. 2012. Thirteen ways of looking at libraries, discovery, and the catalog: Scale, workflow, attention. *EDUCAUSE Review Online* (December 10), http://www.educause.edu/ero/article/thirteen-ways-looking-libraries-discovery-and-catalog-scale-workflow-attention.

De Rosa, Cathy. 2005. *Perceptions of libraries and information resources: A report to the OCLC Membership*. Dublin, OH: OCLC Online Computer Library Center.

Faniel, Ixchel M. 2009. *Unrealized potential: The socio-technical challenges of a large scale cyberinfrastructure initiative*. Arlington, VA: National Science Foundation. http://hdl.handle.net/2027.42/61845.

Faniel, Ixchel, Eric Kansa, Sarah Whitcher Kansa, Julianna Barrera-Gomez, and Elizabeth Yakel. 2013. The challenges of digging data: A study of context in archaeological data reuse. In *JCDL 2013 Proceedings of the 13th ACM/IEEE-CS Joint Conference on Digital Libraries*, 295-304. New York: ACM. http://dx.doi.org/10.1145/2467696.2467712.

Faniel, Ixchel M., and Ann Zimmerman. 2011. Beyond the data deluge: A research agenda for large-scale data sharing and reuse. *International Journal of Digital Curation* 6, no. 1: 58-69. http://www.ijdc.net/index.php/ijdc/article/view/163.

Fast, Karl V., and D. Grant Campbell. 2004. "I still like Google:" University student perceptions of searching OPACs and the web. *Proceedings of the ASIS&T Annual Meeting* 41: 138-46.

Glassmeyer, Sarah. 2010. Ranganathan 2.0. *AALL Spectrum* 14, no. 3: 22-24.

Goldup, Stacey Jeanette. 2010. *Public libraries in the digital age: Investing the implementation of Ranganathan's Five Laws of library science in physical and online library services*. Report submitted to the School of Information Management, Victoria University of Wellington, February 2010.

Gorman, Michael. 1998. The five laws of library science: Then & now. Excerpt of *Our singular strengths*, by Michael Gorman. *School Library Journal* 7: 20-23.

Griffiths, José M., and Donald W. King. 2008. *InterConnections: The IMLS National Study on the Use of Libraries, Museums and the Internet: General information report*. Washington, DC: Institute of Museum and Library Services.

Head, Alison J., and Michael B. Eisenberg. 2009. *Lessons learned: How college students seek information in the digital age*. Project Information Literacy Progress Report, The Information School, University of Washington, http://projectinfolit.org/images/pdfs/pil_fall2009_finalv_yr1_12_2009v2.pdf.

Idaho Commission for Libraries. 2007. *Perceptions of Idaho's digital natives on public libraries: Statewide focus group findings*. Washington, DC: Institute of Museum and Library Services.

Institute for Archaeologists. 2009. *Standard and guidance for the creation, compilation, transfer and deposition of archaeological archives*. n.p.: Institute for Archaeologists. http://www.archaeologists.net/sites/default/files/node-files/Archives2009.pdf.

Kwanya, Tom, Christine Stilwell, and Peter G. Underwood. 2010. Library 2.0 principles and Ranganathan's fifth law. *Mousaion* 28, no. 2: 1-16.

Merriam-Webster.com. Convenience. Accessed December 12, http://www.merriam-webster.com/dictionary/convenience.

Noruzi, Alireza. 2004. Application of Ranganathan's Laws to the web. *Webology* 1, no. 2, http://www.webology.org/2004/v1n2/a8.html.

Oblinger, Diana G., and James L. Oblinger, eds. 2005. *Educating the net generation*. Boulder: EDUCAUSE. http://www.educause.edu/content.asp?PAGE_ID=5989&bhcp=1.

Parks Canada. 2005. *Archaeological recording manual: Excavations and surveys*. n.p.: Parks Canada. http://www.pc.gc.ca/eng/docs/pc/guide/fp-es/titre-title.aspx.

Prabha, Chandra, Lynn Silipigni Connaway, and Timothy J. Dickey. 2006. *Sense-making the information confluence: The whys and hows of college and university user satisficing of information needs. Phase IV: Semi-structured interview study*. Report on National Leadership Grant LG-02-03-0062-03, to Institute of Museum and Library Services, Washington, DC. Columbus, OH: School of Communication, The Ohio State University.

Pullinger, David. 1999. Academics and the new information environment: The impact of local factors on use of electronic journals. *Journal of Information Science* 25, no. 2: 164-72.

Purcell, Kristen, Lee Rainie, Alan Heaps, Judy Buchanan, Linda Friedrich, Amanda Jacklin, Clara Chen, and Kathryn Zickuhr. 2012. *How teens do research in the digital world*. Washington DC: PEW Internet & American Life Project. http://pewinternet.org/Reports/2012/Student-Research.aspx.

Ranganathan, Shiyali Ramamrita. 1931. *The five laws of library science*. London: Edward Goldston, Ltd.

Savolainen, Reijo. 1993. The sense-making theory: Reviewing the interests of a user-centered approach to information seeking and use. *Information Processing & Management* 29, no. 1: 13-28.

Simon, Herbert A. 1957. A behavioral model of rational choice. In *Models of man: Social and rational*. New York: John Wiley & Sons.

Sweeney, Richard. 2006. Millennial behaviors & demographics. http://certi.mst.edu/media/administrative/certi/documents/Article-Millennial-Behaviors.pdf.

Talja, Sanna, Heidi Keso, and Tarja Pietilainen. 1999. The production of "context" in information seeking research: A metatheoretical view. *Information Processing & Management* 35, no. 6: 751-63.

Van Scoyoc, Anna M., and Caroline Cason. 2006. The electronic academic library: Undergraduate research behavior in a library without books. *portal: Libraries and the Academy* 6, no. 1: 47-58.

White, David. 2011. The learning black market. *TALL Blog* (September 30), http://tallblog.conted.ox.ac.uk/index.php/2011/09/30/the-learning-black-market/.

White, David, Lynn Silipigni Connaway, Donna Lanclos, Alison Le Cornu, and Erin Hood. 2012. *Digital Visitors and Residents: Progress report*. Report submitted to Jisc, June 2012. http://www.jisc.ac.uk/media/documents/projects/visitorsandresidentsinterim%20report.pdf.

2

Every person
his or her book.

> " What a volume of ideas rests in a potential state of these six words of but seven syllables! How exacting will be the task of carrying out these ideas!"
> —**Ranganathan 1931, 75**

What's the new second law?
The old second law!

If "save time of the reader" is the new first law in our reordering of Ranganathan's laws, what should be the new second law? In today's environment of information abundance and attention scarcity, the new second law has to be the old second law: "every person his or her book." Clearly, connecting every user who walks through library doors or searches library sites with the precise content they need—be it from one library's collection, the collective collection or the web collection—is of paramount importance in distinguishing libraries from other information service providers in the digital environment. There is no value in saving the time of the reader if we cannot pinpoint the information he or she needs.

Obviously, sweeping, significant change has occurred over the past 83 years, and today the world, as well as the library, is adapting to the impact of a technology revolution as profound as the switch from mainframes to PCs. The environmental forces reshaping the information landscape—search engines, global connectivity, cloud computing, social networking, big data, hand-held and tablet devices, to name but a few—are redefining once again what it means to be a teacher, a scholar, a business person, a student, and a librarian.

Nonetheless, the basic principles of Ranganathan's second law carry well into today's world. In 1931, when he wrote his doctrine, Ranganathan's insistence on "every person" was meant to eliminate restrictions for accessing library collections. The law also was concerned with matching a person's information needs with the library's content, which was primarily books in Ranganathan's day. That's the second part of the law, "his or her book." Ranganathan thought the books in a library collection should be based on and responsive to individual demands, accompanied by a professional, knowledgeable staff ready to guide, navigate and assist the information seeker in the information quest.

Now let's fast forward to the digital, Web-transformed world in which we live, where relationships with patrons, materials and programs are vastly different. How does Ranganathan's second law apply? Rubin (2004, 251) interprets this law first to librarians, who "should have excellent firsthand knowledge of the people to be served," and second to collections, which "should meet the special interests of the community." He also encourages librarians to broadly market and promote library services and collections to attract a diverse group of individuals to access and use them (Rubin 2004).

In this chapter, we will explore the two key concepts of the second law. "Every person" means the library will serve all people in the community. And "his or her book" refers to the content. The library will deliver to every person the content he or she needs. We will discuss the two concepts in their original context, review research as to how they apply in today's world, state our interpretation of the second law in our new digital environment and make some recommendations for how librarians can apply our interpretation to their operations.

Examining the law in today's environment

At its heart, "every person" exudes a strong sense of public purpose, the fervent belief in access to information for all people, which remains a central tenet of librarianship. In fact, the desire by librarians to serve all people has increased in importance in today's digital world, as evidenced by efforts to bring workstations, licensed resources, web content, information literacy and Internet connections to all segments of the population in all parts of the world, even the most remote.

These efforts underscore the importance of available technology, often found at the library, as a critical factor in every person's chance for success. But there's a rub. The context for whom libraries serve and what libraries need on behalf of their communities is shifting. It is being redefined around e-content and a multitude of user segments with differing needs of which librarians are not thoroughly knowledgeable. And in some cases, this lack of knowledge may be driving potential users to other information service providers.

The rise of e-content

Alireza Noruzi (2004) suggests the second law could be "every user his or her web resource." This is easier said than done for libraries. A major challenge in fulfilling this interpretation of the second law is effectively managing the integration of electronic journals, e-books and other e-resources into library collections and making that content discoverable and accessible. Licensed e-content now is the largest collection expenditure for most academic libraries. Locally produced e-content is getting more attention and resources as print collections are moving into a shared environment for management and preservation. Local digital assets and archives are being coordinated with large-scale digital archives. Stewardship of unique assets associated with an institution, such as special collections and research data, are being given increased priority and demand increased resourcing.

It's a lot to juggle, especially when resources are limited and the alternative information service providers are seemingly better, faster and more effective. Libraries also face a challenge with how users perceive libraries' provision of e-content. In one study, researchers were found to "place a very high value on electronic journals, but a much lower value as yet on libraries' provision of other kinds of digital resources" (Consortium of University Research Libraries, and Research Information Network 2007, 39). Several studies have reported that university resources were not the first or second choice among academic communities and often fell behind open access materials (Beetham, McGill, and Littlejohn 2009; Centre for Information Behaviour and the Evaluation of the Research 2008; Connaway and Dickey 2010; Warwick et al. 2008). Similarly, in a 2005 survey, 90% of respondents described a search engine as a "perfect" or "good" fit for their lifestyle, whereas only 49% did so for a library and fewer still for an online library (De Rosa et al. 2005, 3-27-28).

Despite the challenges, we agree with Cloonan and Dove (2005, 59), who write that the second law demands that librarians "eliminate the obstacles that prevent users from making effective use of electronic resources." Clearly, user information behaviors and habits are putting more importance on e-content, e-books and socially-created content than on print resources. The tipping point has occurred and, maybe even more so than in the 1930s, the notion of "every person his or her book" is still important.

Big opportunity in big data

The Association of Research Libraries (ARL), the Association of American Universities (AAU) and The Association of Public and Land-grant Universities (APLU) have partnered around a SHared Access Research Ecosystem (SHARE) initiative. "SHARE's central tenet is that policies expanding public access should provide an opportunity for higher education institutions—individually and collectively—to fulfill their missions to create, disseminate, and preserve knowledge" (Walters and Ruttenberg 2014, 56). Given federal funding agency mandates, federal policies and initiatives within higher education and research communities like SHARE, libraries are increasingly being called upon to manage, curate, and/or preserve massive amounts of digital assets—images, text and data, etc. To facilitate this effort, Erway (2013) calls on library directors to initiate conversations with university stakeholders to develop campus-wide data management policies.

In February 2013, the White House Office of Science and Technology Policy issued a memorandum for science agencies to develop public access policies for research outputs, including publications and data (Holdren 2013). However, studies have indicated that to effectively reuse the data, many different kinds of research outputs have to be captured, such as detailed data collection and coding procedures, detailed descriptions of measurement instruments and tools, data limitations and errors, and information about the researchers and repositories (Faniel and Jacobsen 2010; Faniel et al. 2013; Faniel, Kriesberg, and Yakel 2012; Yakel et al., "Trust in Digital Repositories," 2013). Thus, the growth of digital assets is due to not only what is commonly called the "data deluge" (Hey and Trefethen 2003) but also the need to capture details about various activities that occur upstream as well as downstream in the research lifecycle.

Lavoie et al. (2014) present a framework describing the materials generated during scholarly inquiry now being captured before and after the dissemination of traditional published outcomes and they outline key roles in the stakeholder ecosystem. Even though the role of the academic library in aggregating and servicing these assets for the campus community is still emerging, we are seeing libraries shifting attention from managing a narrowly defined set of materials produced at the end of the research lifecycle to managing a broader range of scholarly outputs produced throughout the research lifecycle. Most are not staffed or structured to do it alone, but they have been taking a leadership role. One of our studies, which examines the early experiences of librarians developing and designing research data services, indicated that librarians have been championing the effort, more than university administration, the office of research, computing services or other units on campus (Faniel, Connaway, and Parson 2014).

> **"**
>
> At [University Name]…the unit in our library that manages our institutional repository and our journal services has traditionally been the place that helps us on data management probably for the last four years, and has worked very closely with faculty and the Office of Research. But, more recently, we've had a lot of conversations about how that can't stay contained in just that group, that it has to spread across our subject specialists librarians in some fashion. So, we're envisioning that all of our subject specialists will have at least some knowledge of data management, and then we'll kind of triage, or we do referrals."
> —**Director, Female, E-Research and Data: Opportunities for Library Engagement**

Librarian-led efforts may be partly attributed to the benefits librarians anticipate gaining for themselves as well as the library (Faniel, Connaway, and Parson 2014). The big opportunities librarians discuss include developing more personal relationships with the researchers and learning more about current research in their subject areas. Several also think providing research data services to faculty and students will help improve service in other aspects of their jobs, such as instruction and collection development. Many others mention that the new services would be just plain fun, interesting and rewarding to provide. In discussing the benefit for the library in particular, librarians think expanding library offerings to include research data services will increase the library's relevance to the campus community.

> "Maybe I'm probably egotistical but I feel like, well, it benefits me, too, because then, my faculty, as a liaison librarian view me as relevant to their research process and come to me or send their students to me more frequently, more readily, I would say. Because they see us as a resource for research and support, in a way that maybe they hadn't connected before. I mean, when I first started... the head faculty was like, 'Oh, I mean I knew you bought books'. And so now, getting that message out, it's just proving value, I think, and that personally is very gratifying."
>
> **—Science Librarian, Female, E-Research and Data: Opportunities for Library Engagement**

Leiden University Libraries has been leading the charge on its campus by proactively defining a new role for librarians to directly engage with the researchers' work. In a presentation at the OCLC Research Libraries Rebound Conference, Kurt de Belder discussed his library's strategic plan to be a "partner in knowledge" and to become the "expert center" for research and teaching. He also described how the library has been gearing up to what they see as key services: virtual research environments, capacities in text and data mining, support for data management and curation, copyright consultation and publication support (De Belder 2012).

The librarians have been conducting in-depth focus groups with faculty to see which of these services are of highest value and where they need additional support. As the librarians move to becoming service experts, they have been allocated time to develop their new skills. Early signs are that the shift has been well received, with an uptake of new services, an emerging reputation of the library as a "go-to" place and the library being included as a partner in developing funding requests (De Belder 2012).

The changing landscape of information-seeking

Adding to the challenges of e-content and digital asset management is the changing landscape of users. Developing and updating collections and services to meet the needs of multiple generations of users with differing approaches to information seeking is tricky to say the least. The different characteristics and information needs of Baby Boomers and Millennials present a dichotomy for library service and system development. Include screenagers, 12—18 year olds (see Rushkoff 1996), graduate students and faculty and the mix becomes even more complex.

The demographics of information seeking. Research indicates that people are more familiar with search engines than with libraries (Connaway Lanclos, and Hood 2013a, 2013b; De Rosa et al. 2005). In an OCLC report, 36% of the survey respondents reported being "extremely familiar" with search engines, 26% reported being "very familiar" with libraries, and 20% percent reported they "have never heard of" online libraries (De Rosa et al. 2005, 1-8). Similarly, a recent Jisc quickguide (2014) reports, "Search engines such as Google, Bing and Yahoo are major discovery tools for all online audiences," and "research repeatedly identifies Google as the main starting point for a wide range of users." Other studies report similar findings, but there also are some differences when demographics are taken into account.

- Google is Millennials' overwhelming first choice for information—for screenagers and graduate students alike. For screenagers, parents and friends are their second choice; graduate students also seek human sources for help, and they include academic superiors among those sources, generally because their research tends to be more sophisticated and exhaustive. Younger Millennials mentioned consulting parents most frequently, while the older Millennials consult friends and professors.

- Baby Boomers indicate that they consult their personal libraries and colleagues. They also read more and use public libraries more than earlier generations. Most of them have Internet access and report that they would miss it if they could no longer use it.

- Undergraduate students (Millennials) tend to seek academic and personal information based on speed and convenience. When describing their information behaviors, they, too, overwhelmingly cited Google as a first choice, with human sources (parents and friends) second.

- Finding online library catalogs difficult to navigate, screenagers use Amazon.com as a discovery tool, and then go the library site. They do consider the authority of electronic sources, but they seem to make many choices based on convenience (cost/benefit), concluding a search when minimum assignment requirements are met.

- Generally more experienced, faculty members reveal yet another stratification in information-seeking patterns. Faculty admitted that they use Google for quick searches, but even there it came in second, behind personal libraries. Their human sources tended to be colleagues or other experts.

The demographics of virtual reference services. Our research indicates some generational differences with virtual reference services (VRS) as well. In general, we can say that for Baby Boomers, problems with VRS tend to be technical. For Millennials, negative issues are more personal. They need more reassurance and want instant answers. Librarians may need to gently let them know that some queries cannot be answered immediately. Boomers are more forgiving than Millennials when more effort is needed to get information. For both, when asked about why they haven't tried VRS, unfamiliarity with it tops the list. They simply did not know it existed.

Screenagers have different communication and information behaviors in the chat reference environment than those of previous generations. Younger Millennials—screenagers—many of whom have been warned about the dangers of anonymous online chat environments, are sometimes apprehensive about VRS chat because they don't know who they are corresponding with, perhaps evil "psycho killers" (Connaway et al. 2008).

Graduate students also worry about being logged into chat rooms, but for a different reason: They worry about chat transcripts being made available to their professors, and they fear negative judgments from librarians and advisors arising from the content of the transcripts.

We also found that users are not as interested in receiving instruction as librarians are in giving it; although they are more receptive in face-to-face (FtF) reference encounters. While willing to wait for good content, they are not necessarily willing to spend the time learning to fish for themselves.

There are some common behaviors demonstrated by older Millennials and the screenagers. The screenagers perceived that asking a follow-up question was "pestering" the librarian, a finding echoed in the older Millennials.

The reduced need for reassurance also demonstrates the Millennials' comfort with chat as a medium for communication, just as the adults' greater need for reassurance may indicate uneasiness with chat.

In short, information-seeking and VRS research suggests that librarians are not necessarily fully cognizant of how faculty and students use library systems or how they view library services. A better understanding the disparities may prove beneficial to discovering ways to integrate library services in user-preferred environments (Calhoun et al. 2009; Connaway and Radford 2011; Connaway and Wakeling 2012).

Our interpretation of the law

As Ranganathan predicted, providing "every person his or her book" is a demanding, exacting task! It requires knowing the information needs and preferences of users in the community and anticipating and matching what they will need in the future. Serving everyone—all people—with content—whatever they need for their education or recreation—requires more care, effort and attention today than ever before.

Going forward in our global, interconnected world, we propose a new interpretation of Ranganathan's second law that keeps its principles intact but recognizes these changes and extends a deeper sense of purpose into the consciousness of information professionals operating in today's Web-dominated world—a rewording in which rich history and tradition combine with advancement and modernization of the newly created library. Our modern day rephrasing of this law is:

Know your community and its needs.

Our intention behind our interpretation of "every person his or her book" is to extend its meaning beyond the people who simply come to the library. Knowing your community and its needs includes those who don't use the library. It also includes virtual users in the proximate and regional geographies as well as other parts of the world. In order to work with other organizations to solve community specific issues, whether poverty, literacy, grant awards or graduation rates, libarians have to understand key community issues and demographic profiles. Knowing the community in-depth will extend the library's reach and widen its circle of influence.

Our interpretation of the law also extends needs beyond physical materials and digital content and delves into the growing demands of the diverse audiences being served, which may require new skills, new services, or new collaborations. For example, needs may range from data management to device support to media expertise. Expanding programs and services to meet some of these new needs will maximize library impact with perhaps some new constituencies who will in turn champion library efforts.

Having a more in-depth understanding of community needs is a critical success factor in today's digital environment where so many information service providers operate. Moreover, community expectations for libraries are being set by experiences with whiz-bang consumer technologies. Failing to embrace these new challenges may drive the community elsewhere and diminish the library's role in content management and delivery.

Librarians are not always fully cognizant of how communities use library systems or how they view library services in part because of the wide range of audiences and demographics—local researchers, students and parents, as well as virtual users, both local and worldwide. Identifying each segment and then knowing, anticipating and supporting their needs requires research, trend watching and analytics. It's also critical to know the strengths and limitations within the library. Developing this dual understanding is what helps librarians discover and make informed decisions about new ways to integrate library services into user-preferred environments.

Recommendations

With the shift and expansion in content and user segments, knowing the needs of the communities being served is challenging. However, if "the mission of librarians is to improve society through facilitating knowledge creation in their communities" (Lankes), then librarians need to become a part of the communities and be more in tune with the dynamics. In the paragraphs that follow, we provide some recommendations that might help.

Approaches to getting to know the library's communities

We start by discussing four approaches for becoming better informed about library communities and their needs: (1) performing traditional outreach, (2) conducting user studies, (3) developing collaborative work relationships with users and (4) running analytics.

1. Traditional outreach allows librarians to keep a pulse on what's happening on a semester, if not monthly or daily, basis through workshop instruction, consultation and reference activities. By gathering data about a community through the questions people ask or advice they seek, librarians develop knowledge. Although the knowledge may not be empirical, it can be used to inform instruction and collection activities and to spot possible trends.

2. User studies provide librarians with a means to take a systematic approach to getting answers to a particular question or problem. For example, how is space being used at the library? What services are used vs. not used? What are the data management, curation and preservation needs of faculty and students on campus? In taking a systematic approach to getting answers to a question, librarians' decisions about whether to launch, redesign or stop offering a particular service are better informed and generalizable to the campus community.

3. Collaborative work relationships with users are more commonly referred to as embedded librarianship. By developing a deep, shared understanding of user needs, librarians can offer customized contributions. This can involve the librarians having offices within the academic departments and being active members of research and teaching teams. Even though the librarian's contributions may be highly sought and valued by the collaborator, the contributions may not be readily generalizable to everyone on campus.

4. Analytics is an application of Big Data. It is the ability to provide forward-looking decision making based on historical data from multiple, disparate data sources. Library service offerings and delivery increasingly will be informed by analytics. In academic libraries, analysis may include using patent applications intersected with current research profiles to advise researchers on future work. Librarians increasingly will need to partner with institutional staff and external organizations to excel at this activity.

All of these approaches yield knowledge about which communities libraries are serving and the needs of the communities, but the knowledge gathered varies. In getting to know communities and their needs, librarians also have to think about how the knowledge can be purposefully applied to improving the library. In doing so, they will be able to choose an approach that suits their objectives.

We provide two examples that describe how librarians are getting to know their communities. The first example discusses ways librarians are informing themselves about the needs of their research communities. The second describes how librarians are learning about the information needs and behaviors of a diverse constituency.

Getting to know research communities and their needs

> 66
>
> There are many different groups in the research community and each has different cultures, approaches, and methods…Not all disciplines share the same language, concepts, or ideals. The culture of the disciplines dictates how and what information is shared, stored, reported, etc."
> —**Connaway and Dickey 2010, 4**

With data management and sharing mandates have come questions from faculty and students who are grappling with issues related to data selection, integrity, storage, accessibility, metadata and documentation and intellectual property concerns, to name a few (Faniel and Zimmerman 2011). Librarians have the experience and expertise to help researchers in these areas, but they must make a concerted effort to learn more about the researchers' needs and challenges.

Determine the why of the issue. Simply knowing the issues the community is facing is not enough. Librarians must know from the researchers' perspective, why the community is facing a particular issue. Is it related to limited tools and technologies, disincentives for data management and sharing, cultural or social factors? Understanding the why of an issue is particularly important since the reasons may vary across disciplines.

Some disciplines are better motivated and organized to share and reuse each others' data. The data collection equipment may be too expensive or the amount and/or diversity of data required to answer the research question may be more than an individual can collect alone. In these instances researchers are scientifically motivated to share and reuse each others' data; the research cannot advance otherwise.

In other disciplines, cultural and social factors make for slow progress toward data sharing and reuse. For instance, researchers may be in competition to make the first discoveries, have intellectual property concerns or want to protect graduate students' interests (Campbell et al. 2002; Griffiths 2008; Sayogo and Prado 2012; Tenopir et al. 2011).

Assess and reflect local needs. "Changes in the research libraries must be driven by and reflect the needs of the research communities they seek to support" (Luce 2008, 48). Since the beginning, librarians have been needs focused, whether examining behaviors and attitudes toward data management and sharing, developing data curation profiles and design personas, understanding education requirements or gauging individuals' interest for getting help from librarians (Delserone 2008; Lage, Losoff, and Maness 2011; Research Information Network 2008; Scaramozzino,

Ramirez, and McGaughey 2012; Witt et al. 2009). However, we propose that librarians focus their engagement with faculty and students in three key ways: (1) start farther upstream in the research cycle at the point when researchers are planning their studies, (2) focus attention on the research processes as well as the research products and (3) consider the perspectives of those reusing as well as those producing the data.

Increasingly, librarians have been inserting themselves into faculty and student data management planning processes prior to grant submission. We suggest insertion continue after the grant is awarded. The focus should then shift to understanding how the research unfolds and how the data are generated and documented with respect to the researchers' workflows. Librarians should also consider the perspective of data reusers. People producing data have different needs and work-flows than people reusing data. Morever, understanding the needs of data reusers is particularly important for preserving the meaning of data (Faniel and Yakel 2011). There may be worry about being obtrusive. Working in such close proximity is unique and novel, but so are the challenges of large-scale data sharing and reuse. We are still learning about them, and new challenges like these often require new approaches in order to be addressed effectively. Librarians should observe, learn from and collaborate with faculty and students, whatever they will allow, in order to help them meet their needs. Engagement with faculty and students has to occur on a deeper level with an objective to gain firsthand knowledge about the research, the data, and the challenges of data management, curation and preservation.

Getting to know the needs of a diverse constituency

> " We have little understanding of what motivates individuals to use particular technologies or spaces when engaging with the information environment. As a result people tend to adopt simplistic but culturally panicked ideas in their attempts to grasp the problem while others delve into specifics to the extent that little substantive conclusions can be drawn."
> —Connaway, White, and Lanclos 2011, 1

The academic community reflects diverse groups from Millennials to Baby Boomers, who bring with them different mental models from very different perspectives. Millennials have never lived without computers, the Internet, or remote controls for televisions. This does not mean that Millennials are more technological savvy than older individuals.

Research indicates that age is but one factor in determining how individuals discover, select, access and use resources and engage with technology. Other factors include educational stage, discipline, experience and socio-economic factors (Connaway, Lanclos, and Hood 2013a, 2013b; Connaway, Lanclos et al. 2013; Faniel 2012; Yakel et al., "Archaeological Data," 2013; Yakel et al., "Trust in Digital Repositories," 2013). In order to provide "every person his or her book," librarians must know the needs of their community.

Determine the why of the issue. Simply acknowledging that the academic community has diverse habits and needs won't help librarians develop information services that will be trusted and used. Librarians must first understand why people use the information services and resources. This involves actively engaging with the academic community's teaching, learning and research endeavors. Engaging with faculty and students by attending classes, providing help with finding information sources for projects and becoming an active member of the projects is an excellent opportunity for discovering why they use specific information services and resources.

To understand the disciplinary communities they serve in a larger context, librarians should consider meeting to discuss their experiences. They can work together to synthesize the similarities and differences they are observing when working with users across the demographic groups. This information could then be used to brainstorm solutions that can be generalized to larger segments of the campus community as well as approaches that stay true to the unique needs of a discipline.

Assess and reflect local needs. It is important for libraries to focus on those who are familiar to them because they use their facilities and services, but librarians also should consider non-users. Working more closely with students and faculty as part of a course is one way to do this. However, the simple act of convening a discussion among the different demographic groups within the academic community can provide insights and a deeper understanding of how they get their information, why they choose it, and what information services they need to be effective.

Focus groups are particularly useful not only for reaching students and getting their feedback but also for introducing them to different understandings of knowledge and how it is established within cultures and communities. An awareness of the difference between knowledge as memorized or captured information and knowledge as a socially-constructed phenomenon should offer them greater choices in information seeking, as well as validate a range of approaches to learning which are open to them. Convening a cross-disciplinary group of faculty to discuss the opportunities and challenges they experience in research and teaching may uncover common concerns, needs and approaches across the disciplines. Librarians could then use the information gathered as a basis for developing policies, services and processes that would better serve larger segments of the community.

Conclusion

Ranganathan's second law is clearly applicable today and carries with it an expanded charge in the new digital environment in which libraries are operating. "Every person his or her book" is now know your community and its needs, with the reinterpretation calling for new services from libraries and new skills from librarians along with continuing the key practices of today.

Knowing your community and its needs is a key step in developing these new programs and moving in new directions will help libraries remain transformational places, as central to our shared future as they have been to our shared past. The needs of the 21st century demand that librarians, who serve the public good, develop new habits and mindsets to go along with the traditional roles they have played. It is imperative to expand and extend the library's presence in the community by delivering new, needed services to changing user groups.

Now more than ever, we make the case for investment in our libraries by the moral force of their work—the openness they represent, the sharing they undertake and the innovation they implement.

Moving from "every person his or her book" to know your community and its needs presents an opportunity to bring considerable value to our communities through leadership, collaboration and a range of supporting services. Rich history and tradition combine with advancement and modernization at the newly created library.

References

Beetham, Helen, Lou McGill, and Allison Littlejohn. 2009. *Thriving in the 21st century: Learning Literacies for the Digital Age (LLiDA Project)*. Glasgow: The Caledonian Academy, Glasgow Caledonian University. http://www.academy.gcal.ac.uk/llida/LLiDAReportJune2009.pdf.

Calhoun, Karen, Joanne Cantrell, Peggy Gallagher, and Janet Hawk. 2009. *Online catalogs: What users and librarians want: An OCLC report*. Dublin, OH: OCLC.

Campbell, Eric G., Brian R. Clarridge, Manjusha Gokhale, Lauren Birenbaum, Stephen Hilgartner, Neil A. Holtzman, and David Blumenthal. 2002. Data withholding in academic genetics: Evidence from a national survey. *JAMA: The Journal of the American Medical Association* 287, no. 4: 473-80.

Centre for Information Behaviour and the Evaluation of Research. 2008. *Information behaviour of the researcher of the future: A CIBER briefing paper*. London: CIBER.

Cloonan, Michele V., and John G. Dove. 2005. Ranganathan online: Do digital libraries violate the Third Law? *Library Journal* 130, no. 6: 58-60.

Connaway, Lynn Silipigni, and Timothy J. Dickey. 2010. *The digital information seeker: Report of findings from selected OCLC, RIN, and JISC user behavior projects*. n.p.: Higher Education Funding Council for England (HEFCE). http://www.jisc.ac.uk/media/documents/publications/reports/2010/digitalinformationseekerreport.pdf.

Connaway, Lynn Silipigni, Donna Lanclos, and Erin M. Hood. 2013a. "I always stick with the first thing that comes up on Google…" Where people go for information, what they use, and why. *EDUCAUSE Review Online* (December 6), http://www.educause.edu/ero/article/i-always-stick-first-thing-comes-google-where-people-go-information-what-they-use-and-why.

Connaway, Lynn Silipigni, Donna Lanclos, and Erin M. Hood. 2013b. "I find Google a lot easier than going to the library website." Imagine ways to innovate and inspire students to use the academic library. *Proceedings of the Association of College & Research Libraries (ACRL) 2013 conference, April 10-13, 2013, Indianapolis, IN.* Chicago: Association of College & Research Libraries. http://www.ala.org/acrl/sites/ala.org.acrl/files/content/conferences/confsandpreconfs/2013/papers/Connaway_Google.pdf.

Connaway, Lynn Silipigni, Donna Lanclos, David White, Alison Le Cornu, and Erin M. Hood. 2013. User-centered decision making: A new model for developing academic library services and systems. *IFLA Journal* 39, no. 1: 30-36.

Connaway, Lynn Silipigni, and Marie L. Radford. 2011. *Seeking synchronicity: Revelations and recommendations for virtual reference.* Dublin, OH: OCLC Research. http://www.oclc.org/reports/synchronicity/full.pdf.

Connaway, Lynn Silipigni, Marie L. Radford, Timothy J. Dickey, Jocelyn De Angelis Williams, and Patrick Confer. 2008. Sense-making and synchronicity: Information-seeking behaviors of Millennials and Baby Boomers. *Libri* 58, no. 2: 123-35. http://www.oclc.org/resources/research/publications/library/2008/connaway-libri.pdf.

Connaway, Lynn Silipigni, and Simon Wakeling. 2012. *To use or not to use WorldCat.org: An international perspective from different user groups.* Unpublished report, April 26.

Connaway, Lynn Silipigni, David White, and Donna Lanclos. 2011. Visitors and Residents: What motivates engagement with the digital information environment? *Proceedings of the 74th ASIS&T Annual Meeting* 48: 1-7.

Consortium of University Research Libraries, and Research Information Network. 2007. *Researchers' use of academic libraries and their services: A report.* London: Research Information Network and Consortium of University Research Libraries. http://www.rin.ac.uk/our-work/using-and-accessing-informationresources/researchers-use-academic-libraries-and-their-serv.

Dasgupta, Arjun. 2007. "Library staff" and Ranganathan's Five Laws. *IASLIC Bulletin* 52, no. 4: 195-204.

De Belder, Kurt. 2012. Session 1: Directly supporting researchers. Presented at Libraries rebound: Embracing mission, maximizing impact, June 5-6, in Philadelphia, PA. https://www.youtube.com/watch?v=R9qUoVSD7HA&feature=youtu.be.

Delserone, Leslie M. 2008. At the watershed: Preparing for research data management and stewardship at the University of Minnesota Libraries. *Library Trends* 57, no. 2: 202-210.

De Rosa, Cathy, Joanne Cantrell, Diane Cellentani, Janet Hawk, Lillie Jenkins, and Alane Wilson. 2005. *Perceptions of libraries and information resources: A report to the OCLC Membership.* Dublin, OH: OCLC Online Computer Library Center.

Erway, Ricky. 2013. *Starting the conversation: University-wide research data management policy.* Dublin, OH: OCLC Research. http://www.oclc.org/content/dam/research/publications/library/2013/2013-08.pdf.

Faniel, Ixchel M. 2012. Infusing consumer data reuse practices into curation and preservation activities. Presented at the 76th Annual Meeting of the Society of American Archivists (SAA), August 11, in San Diego, CA. http://files.archivists.org/conference/sandiego2012/504-Faniel.pdf.

Faniel, Ixchel, Lynn Silipigni Connaway, and Kendra Parson. 2014. 20th Annual Reference Research Forum. Presented at ALA Annual Conference & Exhibition, June 26-July 1, in Las Vegas, NV.

Faniel, Ixchel M., and Trond E. Jacobsen. 2010. Reusing scientific data: How earthquake engineering researchers assess the reusability of colleagues' data. *Computer Supported Cooperative Work* 19, no. 3-4: 355-75.

Faniel, Ixchel, Eric Kansa, Sarah Whitcher Kansa, Julianna Barrera-Gomez, and Elizabeth Yakel. 2013. The challenges of digging data: A study of context in archaeological data reuse. In *JCDL 2013 Proceedings of the 13th ACM/IEEE-CS Joint Conference on Digital Libraries*, 295-304. New York: ACM. http://dx.doi.org/10.1145/2467696.2467712.

Faniel, Ixchel M., Adam Kriesberg, and Elizabeth Yakel. 2012. Data reuse and sensemaking among novice social scientists. Paper presented at the annual meeting of the American Society for Information Science and Technology, October 26-31, in Baltimore, MD.

Faniel, Ixchel M., and Elizabeth Yakel. 2011. Significant properties as contextual metadata. *Journal of Library Metadata* 11: 155-65.

Faniel, Ixchel M., and Ann Zimmerman. 2011. Beyond the data deluge: A research agenda for large-scale data sharing and reuse. *International Journal of Digital Curation* 6, no. 1: 58-69. http://www.ijdc.net/index.php/ijdc/article/view/163.

Gorman, Michael. 1998. The five laws of library science: Then & now. Excerpt of *Our singular strengths*, by Michael Gorman. *School Library Journal* 7: 20-23.

Griffiths, Aaron. 2008. The publication of research data: Researcher attitudes and behavior. *The International Journal of Digital Curation* 4, no. 1: 46-56. http://www.ijdc.net/index.php/ijdc/issue/view/7.

Hey, Tony, and Anne Trefethen. 2003. The data deluge: An e-science perspective. In *Grid computing: Making the global information infrastructure a reality*, edited by Fran Berman, Geoffrey Fox, and Tony Hey, 809-824. Chichester, UK: Wiley.

Holdren, John P. 2013. Memorandum for the heads of executive departments and agencies. Washington, DC: Office of Science and Technology Policy. http://www.whitehouse.gov/sites/default/files/microsites/ostp/ostp_public_access_memo_2013.pdf.

Jisc. 2014. Make your digital resources easier to discover. Quickguide. http://www.jisc.ac.uk/guides/make-your-digital-resources-easier-to-discover.

Kwanya, Tom, Christine Stilwell, and Peter G. Underwood. 2010. Library 2.0 principles and Ranganathan's Fifth Law. *Mousaion* 28, no. 2: 1-16.

Lage, Kathryn, Barbara Losoff, and Jack Maness. 2011. Receptivity to library involvement in scientific data curation: A case study at the University of Colorado Boulder. *portal: Libraries and the Academy* 11, no. 4: 915-37.

Lankes, R. David, blog. The atlas of new librarianship. http://www.newlibrarianship.org/wordpress/.

Lavoie, Brian, Eric Childress, Ricky Erway, Ixchel Faniel, Constance Malpas, Jennifer Schaffner, and Titia van der Werf. 2014. *The evolving scholarly record*. Dublin, OH: OCLC Research. http://www.oclc.org/research/publications/library/2014/oclcresearch-evolving-scholarly-record-2014.pdf.

Luce, Richard E. 2008. A new value equation challenge: The emergence of eResearch and roles for research libraries. In *No brief candle: Reconceiving research libraries for the 21st century*. Washington, DC: Council on Library and Information Resources

Noruzi, Alireza. 2004. Application of Ranganathan's Laws to the web. *Webology* 1, no. 2, http://www.webology.org/2004/v1n2/a8.html.

OCLC Research. User behavior studies & synthesis. OCLC. http://oclc.org/research/activities/ubs.html.

Ranganathan, Shiyali Ramamrita. 1931. *The five laws of library science*. London: Edward Goldston, Ltd.

Research Information Network. 2008. *To share or not to share: Publication and quality assurance of research data outputs*. London: Research Information Network.

Rubin, Richard E. 2004. *Foundations of library and information science*. New York: Neal-Schuman Publishers.

Rushkoff, Douglas. 1996. *Playing the future: How kids' culture can teach us to thrive in an age of chaos*. New York: HarperCollins.

Sayogo, Djoko Sigit, and Theresa A. Pardo. 2012. Exploring the motive for data publication in open data initiative: Linking intention to action. *2012 45th Hawaii International Conference on System Sciences*.

Scaramozzino, Jeanine Marie, Marisa L. Ramirez, and Karen J. McGaughey. 2012. A study of faculty data curation behaviors and attitudes at a teaching-centered university. *College & Research Libraries* 73, no. 4: 349-65. http://crl.acrl.org/content/73/4/349.full.pdf+html.

Tenopir, Carol, Suzie Allard, Kimberly Douglass, Arsev Umur Aydinoglu, Lei Wu, Eleanor Read, Maribeth Manoff, and Mike Frame. 2011. Data sharing by scientists: Practices and perceptions. *PLoS ONE* 6, no. 6: e21101. http://www.plosone.org/article/info%3Adoi%2F10.1371%2Fjournal.pone.0021101.

Walters, Tyler, and Judy Ruttenberg. 2014. Shared access research ecosystem. *EDUCAUSE Review Online* 49, no. 2: 56-57. http://www.educause.edu/ero/article/shared-access-research-ecosystem.

Warwick, Claire, Isabel Galina, Melissa Terras, Paul Huntington, and Nikoleta Pappa. 2008. The Master Builders: LAIRAH research on good practice in the construction of digital humanities projects. *Literary and Linguistic Computing* 23, no. 3: 383-96. http://discovery.ucl.ac.uk/13810/.

Witt, Michael, Jacob Carlson, D. Scott Brandt, and Melissa Cragin. 2009. Constructing data curation profiles. *The International Journal of Digital Curation* 4, no. 3: 93-103.

Yakel, Elizabeth, Ixchel Faniel, Eric Kansa, and Sara Whitcher Kansa. 2013. Archaeological data: Curation, preservation, and reuse. Presented at the Society for American Archaeology (SAA) 78th Annual Meeting, April 3-7, in Honolulu, HI. http://www.slideshare.net/oclcr/digital-archaeological-data-curation-preservation-and-reuse.

Yakel, Elizabeth, Ixchel Faniel, Adam Kriesberg, and Ayoung Yoon. 2013. Trust in digital repositories. *The International Journal of Digital Curation* 8, no. 1, http://www.ijdc.net/index.php/ijdc/article/view/8.1.143/303.

3

Books are for use.

> " [The] tendency to hoard books must have originated at a time when books were rare and difficult to produce. Before the invention of printing, it took years to copy a book. It is said that the copying of the Mahabharata was work for a whole lifetime. Under such conditions, there was justification for forgetting that BOOKS ARE FOR USE and for overdoing the act of preserving them. But this tendency appears to have unfortunately developed into a regular instinct, as a result of a long practice. Although the situation was thoroughly altered by the invention of printing, it took centuries to overcome this long-inherited habit. The first step was to declare an amnesty for the books and set them free from their chains."
>
> **—Ranganathan 1931, 337**

The new third law: Books are for use

Ranganathan's declaration that "books are for use" was meant to sound an alarm that a radical shift from preservation to use could not occur without key librarian actions and behaviors, such as providing comfortable space, convenient library hours and locations, and knowledgeable staff who offer excellent customer service. Users take these things for granted today; in 1931, they were the exception. Today, libraries are customer focused and offer a much wider range of content, systems and services than in Ranganathan's day, when the emphasis was primarily books and book lending. That's not to say that service, hours, buildings and furniture aren't still important—they are crucial.

Librarians are expected to evaluate wide ranging, constantly changing content and service offerings to ensure users' needs are being met and library materials are being made accessible. Operating in an increasingly complex information and technology infrastructure, librarians must provide proactive, reliable service (Connaway, Dickey, and Radford 2011) and must connect with users in the building and on the Internet. Librarians also must constantly communicate changes in the collections and the access channels to the collections and services so that current and prospective users know how to reach the library and what resources exist beyond books.

In this chapter, we discuss the opportunities and challenges of rethinking and expanding the physical and technical infrastructure—the bricks and mortar facility and the browser-based digital doorway—to extend access beyond books and to boost the library's impact in the digital era.

Examining the law in today's environment

Four simple words, "books are for use," elicit a wide range of commentary from scholars and thought leaders on what Ranganathan really meant in 1931 and its contemporary relevance. Some emphasize the service role of the librarian, whereas others focus on the evolution of newer resource formats and delivery mechanisms (Barner 2011; Bhatt 2011; Cloonan and Dove 2005; Glassmeyer 2010; Goldup 2010; Gorman 1998; Kwanya, Stilwell, and Underwood 2010; Noruzi 2004; Walter 2012).

Service sets books free

Carr makes a case that Ranganathan's first law "is, in effect, declaring that a library is a technology" (Carr 2014, 159). Dasgupta reminds us that Ranganathan set high expectations for the level of service from library staff—welcoming, always courteous and possessing "the ability to understand human nature" (Dasgupta 2007, 201). Gorman stresses the underlying psychological influences prevalent among librarians with emphasis on service to humanity. He noted that "the dominant ethic of librarianship is service to the individual, community and society as a whole... and implies an attention to quality, a desire to...surpass the expectations of library users" (Gorman 1995, 784).

> "
> There's a certain sort of, I don't know a certain sort of nice feeling about going into a library and picking a book off the shelf and going and sitting down and reading it."
> —**UK Undergraduate Student #11, Male, Age 33, Education, Digital Visitors and Residents**

Books themselves—while a smaller fish in an expanding ocean of knowledge resources—still matter. The perception of books as the brand of the modern library endures. In a national survey of Americans 16 years or older, 80% responded that borrowing books is a "very important" service libraries provide and 73% who had visited a library or bookmobile in the last year did so to borrow print books (Zickuhr, Rainie, and Purcell 2013, 3, 6). This also has been echoed by students and faculty when discussing the importance of academic libraries in providing access to books and physical facilities (Connaway, Lanclos, and Hood 2013; Connaway and Radford 2011; Connaway, White et al. 2013; De Rosa et al. 2005; De Rosa et al. 2010; Prabha, Connaway, and Dickey 2006).

Books are still the brand

The law "books are for use" "encapsulates the essence of libraries" (Kwanya, Stilwell, and Underwood 2010, 4). When people mention libraries, they tend to mention books or obtaining them from the library (Connaway, Lanclos, and Hood 2013; Connaway and Radford 2011; Connaway, White et al. 2013; Prabha, Connaway, and Dickey 2006). The perception of books as the library brand has increased by 6% in five years (2005—2010) with 75% of Americans saying books are what come to mind first when they think about a library (De Rosa et al. 2010). This indicates that books and book lending still are very important. However, as librarians continue to extend their content and service offerings, they must be careful that the library isn't identified only as a source and provider of books.

> "People are really, really wedded to the idea that...we're, I mean, still about books. I mean, sure, online journals, but for some reason, it doesn't occur to them that information comes in different packages. It doesn't have to be a book. Hey, we had scrolls too, all different kinds of things. So, now, it's [data in] a spreadsheet or whatever."
> —**Program Director: Science, Engineering, Social Science and Business, Female, E-Research and Data: Opportunities for Library Engagement**

Move beyond books: e-content and improved access are key

Of course, libraries have never been about just books. At the time of Ranganathan's writing, books were not the only materials libraries collected; his point was not about books per se but about acquiring and making materials available for use (Gorman 1998). Current scholars emphasize this point, going so far as to replace the word "books" with terms that encompass the variety of content available, such as "information," "online resources," and "web resources" (Cloonan and Dove 2005; Glassmeyer 2010; Noruzi 2004). The latter terms speak to the growing importance of digital content. E-journals have become increasingly important for academic research (Connaway and Dickey 2010). These days, users—academics in particular—expect everything to be accessible online and are easily frustrated when something is not (Research Information Network 2006, 5).

> "Librarians must increasingly consider a greater variety of digital formats and content. This goes beyond the e-journal revolution to include the curation of data sets, and the providing of emerging services such as VREs [Virtual Research Environments], open source materials, non-text-based and multi-media objects, blogs, and digital resources which have not yet been envisioned."
> —**Connaway and Dickey 2010, 46**

In response to a pop-up survey on WorldCat.org, 36% of survey participants believed "having more links to online content/full text" would be the "most helpful" change to identify a needed item in a catalog (Calhoun et al. 2009, 13). The digital content extends beyond e-journals and e-books to collections that contain such things as older literature, sheet music, art images, biological specimens, archaeological finds and scientific research data (Connaway, Prabha, and Dickey 2006; Faniel and Jacobsen 2010; Faniel et al. 2013). Yet, it remains difficult for users to see past books to other materials the library makes available, including the services librarians have developed to capture, preserve, discover and access these materials. The perception of libraries and librarians has remained largely traditional even though they can and are doing so much more.

Research data are for use

Research data are a perfect example. Driven in part by demands to increase access to the results of federally funded research and by a desire to meet the changing needs of the campus community, librarians have begun to develop services to ensure research data are for use (e.g., Choudhury 2008, 2010; Delserone 2008; Johnston and Hanson 2010; Newton, Miller, and Bracke 2010; Peters and Dryden 2011). The services are often aligned with key skills researchers need when collecting, organizing, processing and analyzing data, including documentation of procedures, ethics and attribution in terms of copyright, intellectual property, confidentiality and privacy of human subjects, data description (metadata) and preservation (Carlson et al. 2011; Carlson, Johnston, Westra, and Nichols 2013; Jahnke, Asher, and Keralis 2012; Johnston and Jeffryes 2013). Librarians are helping to develop researcher skills through traditional service delivery models, such as instruction and consultation, as well as new models in which librarians are more deeply engaged in collaboration with researchers and their work (Auckland 2012; Faniel, Connaway, and Parson 2014).

> " It's kind of what we've always done but I think trying to position ourselves to be more engaged with faculty and be a partner, or like a strong assistant with faculty and meeting their needs, and the library re-envisioning itself as rather than you come to us, we come to you."
> —**Scholarly Communications Librarian, Male, E-Research and Data: Opportunities for Library Engagement**

Research data services: The new cataloging

In an Association of College and Research Libraries (ACRL) survey, library directors reported research data services currently being offered or planned including: finding and citing data sets (65.9%), creating web guides and finding aids (55.9%), developing data management plans (42.7%), assisting with data and metadata (41.7%), and participating in research teams (40.6%). The study reports that instructional and consultative services are more popular than technical services, such as providing support for repositories or discovery and access systems, identifying and preparing data for deposit or deaccessioning data from repositories (Tenopir, Birch, and Allard 2012).

A study of Association of Research Libraries (ARL) member institutions shows similar results. Finding relevant data (83%) and developing data management plans (79%) are current services being provided by librarians. However, for the ARL member institutions, finding and using available technology and infrastructure tools (76%) and developing tools to assist researchers (76%) also are provided (Soehner, Steeves, and Ward 2010).

Similar to Ranganathan, who argued that books should be freely available to all, contemporary scholars are calling to make all content openly, freely and easily accessible when and where needed (Cloonan and Dove 2005; Glassmeyer 2010; Noruzi 2004). As libraries have moved beyond books and have worked to create better access to physical and digital materials, librarians have had to rethink the infrastructure along with their services to keep up with changing times.

Building an infrastructure for access and engagement

Ranganathan stressed improvements to different aspects of the physical infrastructure, such as library location, hours of operation, space, furniture and staff education and training, because he believed they would improve access to library materials. Offering a modern, attractive facility with adequate power, comfortable seating, meeting room space and good acoustical design addressed the community's needs. The same holds true today, but librarians also must actively manage users' social engagement with experts and peers in virtual environments as well as face-to-face (FtF).

Design space for change. Let's start with physical space. Information commons (or learning commons) at the University of Southern California and the University of Iowa in the 1990s were early attempts to provide technology-enabled spaces where students could collaborate and seek help from library and computer services staff (Lippincott 2010). As they have evolved to support collaborative exchanges and social constructions of learning, we also have learned how quickly users' needs change based on their assignments or the demands of the school year (Lippincott 2010). Since there is no one-size-fits-all approach, more recent reconfigurations of space have emphasized flexibility in the face of changing and, at times, competing user needs (Pierard and Lee 2011; Sadler 2012). Students still need spaces for individual contemplation in the face of group work and they still want desktops, even though they have laptops and other mobile technologies (Lippincott 2010; Pierard and Lee 2011; Sadler 2012). Therefore, space has to be designed to be changed.

Break the mold with 'BLAST'. Other reconfigurations emphasize experimentation and take a learn-by-doing approach, which also can be beneficial as it allows for fast implementation of an idea while leaving room to improve as it is used. For the University of North Carolina at Charlotte, the 11-day final exam period was "a key time to support—and engage—stressed students" (Hiebert and Theriault 2012, 540). A committee of nine library staff and faculty members implemented changes to space and activities to BLAST the stress from students, including:

- Bouncing ball activities, such as ping-pong and indoor sponge basketball;

- Lounging opportunities in comfortable seating and low tables;

- Art activities with coloring books, Play-Doh® and puzzles

- Sleep time, including disposable pillows; and

- Touch with therapy dogs to cuddle and pet.

BLAST presents quite a different picture of the academic library. But that's the point. "In effect, space is shifting from infrastructure to engagement, as it supports social interaction around learning and research, access to specialist equipment, expertise or communication facilities exhibitions, and so on" (Dempsey 2012, 11-12).

Stacks are out, people are in. Makerspaces or creativity spaces are another example. They are places where students can access specialist equipment to build, create and craft. By providing physical space and tools, people can share resources and knowledge while engaging in hands-on experimentation (Fisher 2012). "Makerspaces allow students to take control of their own learning as they take ownership of projects they have not just designed but defined" (EDUCAUSE Learning Initiative 2013).

> "
>
> Indeed the Maker Movement and makerspaces aren't something for just those in the engineering or computer science or design departments. They aspire to be openly democratic and participatory. That is one of their great beauties. Steve Jobs once said that Apple's innovation was a result of the company's existence at the intersection of technology and the liberal arts. With that in mind, I'd argue that we can do more to situate colleges and universities at that intersection too—not by buying iPads and certainly not by scrapping the humanities but by welcoming the maker ethos onto our campuses."
>
> **—Watters 2013**

At DeLaMare Science and Engineering Library at the University of Nevada in Reno, moving low-use print items to an automated storage and retrieval facility, covering walls with whiteboard paint, and investing in electronics prototyping kits and 3D printers helped to create a makerspace that increased hourly head counts from 24 to 200 students and increased faculty engagement with the library (American Libraries Editors 2013). In the Wheaton Autonomous Learning Lab (WHALE Lab), an interdisciplinary community of students come together to create a range of output through embroidery, welding and sculpting (EDUCAUSE Learning Initiative 2013). The makerspace at the Odum Library at Valdosta State University provides programming and engineering tools and server space (Fisher 2012; Odum Library 2014). In these instances, librarians stepped outside the box and welcomed new forms of information access and sharing, values core to their identity. As a result, they are sparking innovation in education as well as a change in student and faculty perceptions of the library.

Be ready to change user perceptions and breakthrough barriers. While the broadened view of infrastructure and novel approaches to reimagining it are necessary, such actions are not without challenges. As discussed previously, a major challenge is that users may not know the range of skills and services librarians can offer. Another is users not recognizing that the services they do value are courtesy of the library—particularly the online services that libraries offer.

Studies report that college and university students and faculty who value online library catalogs and databases such as LexisNexis, PubMed and Medline (Prabha, Connaway, and Dickey 2006) don't associate them with the library (Connaway and Radford 2011; Connaway, White et al. 2013; De Rosa et al. 2005; De Rosa et al. 2010; Prabha, Connaway, and Dickey 2006). Failure to acknowledge the role librarians have in the online information-seeking process diminishes the value of library services.

In other cases, the use and adoption of library systems and services is an issue. The first wave of institutional repositories remained practically empty given social, organizational and technical barriers, including a poor understanding of faculty and student motivations and incentives (Nelson 2009; Salo 2008). Disciplinary data repositories face similar barriers (Faniel 2009; Van House 2002; Van House, Butler, and Schiff 1998). For research data specifically, the reasons faculty and students hesitate, limit or refuse when asked to share their data include: limited or poor tools and technical support, no place to put the data, lack of time and funding to prepare the data, fear of getting scooped, fear of not getting credit for sharing, worry that data will be misused or misinterpreted, limited expertise in data management, not knowing what data to share or how to share the data and legal and ethical constraints (Carlson and Stowell-Bracke 2013; Connaway and Dickey 2010; Cragin et al. 2010; Nelson 2009; Research Information Network 2008; Tenopir et al. 2011; Sayogo and Pardo 2012).

With an understanding of why the first wave of institutional repositories failed, several colleges and universities have since incorporated institutional repositories into their research data services offering (Choudhury 2008; Witt 2008). Whether institutional repositories will be widely adopted and used for such purposes remains unclear. Cragin and colleagues (2010) suggest informing the development of institutional repositories with studies of the adoption of other types of repositories. For instance, a study of three digital data repositories show how organizational differences and the varied needs of repository users influence how staff manage change to data collections (Daniels et al. 2012).

Studies of disciplinary data repositories also show that trust plays a role in the extent to which data are shared and reused (Van House 2002; Yakel et al., "Trust in Digital Repositories," 2013; Yoon 2013). Specifically, perceptions of the user community play a key role in determining the trustworthiness of repositories (Prieto 2009; Ross and McHugh 2006). In the case of CalFlora, being able to influence the type of metadata captured facilitated a disciplinary community's trust in the repository (Van House 2002). In another study, archaeologists and social scientists were found to associate trust in data repositories with repository functions (e.g., data processing and selection, metadata creation), institutional actions (e.g., identifying and being transparent with users), assurances (e.g., guarantees of preservation and sustainability, institutional reputation) and endorsements from colleagues (Yakel et al., "Trust in Digital Repositories," 2013).

Our interpretation of the law

Ranganathan promoted the use of books and other library resources when the practice at the time was to store and preserve them. He was not against the storage and preservation of books, but he believed these activities should be conducted in order to make the resources available for individuals to use them.

We believe it's safe to say that the core meaning of "books are for use" is about access, and access remains a key issue more than 80 years since it first was identified by Ranganathan. It remains viable because of the ever-expanding body of materials in physical and digital formats and the growth in the number of channels through which users obtain them. The increase in library substitutes has impacted how users engage with the library. Today, freeing books from their chains takes on new meaning. Our interpretation of the law is:

> ***Develop the physical and technical infrastructure needed to deliver physical and digital materials.***

It's not just the availability of physical and digital materials that matters, but more so the infrastructure—both physical and technical—that libraries put in place to capture and deliver them. Let's face it, today's users often lack awareness of library offerings, whether materials, technology, or services. The lack of awareness seems to rise in parallel with the increase in library substitutes. There also are users who are accessing materials but don't realize the materials are being made available by the library. How can librarians build user awareness? One way is through a revamped physical and technical infrastructure.

Redesigned space—both online and offline—means traffic

Much of today's world is based on social engagement, both FtF and virtual, which means that librarians must develop engaging spaces and connections in both environments. With so many access channels at users' fingertips, librarians must battle for users' attention, so capturing it is the first step. Redesigning physical space in the library to offer creative areas open to the research and learning community has been one tactic. Purposefully redesigned spaces are what get people in the door. When they are in the library, Herbert and Theriault (2012, 546) believe for students in particular, "the message must be clear: the library is genuinely invested in student success and offers the personnel, spaces, technology, and services to achieve it."

Once in the door, opportunities naturally present themselves to ramp up users' awareness of the physical and digital resources available in and accessible through the library. There are opportunities to introduce them to new equipment and technologies and to provide assistance during use. There are opportunities to cultivate social engagements that act to awaken users' perceptions of libraries and librarians. Relationships begin to form, which make way for the introduction and uptake of an ever-evolving portfolio of library offerings geared to meet users' needs, some of which the users may not yet know they need.

Providing engaging virtual spaces is more than simply creating a library website or Facebook page. It must be a welcoming and active environment to entice people to use and engage with both librarians and other users. It also must be obvious to users that they are engaging with the library, its community and materials. As online users link from Instagram to Facebook to the online library catalog to LexisNexis on their way to discovering what they want or need, librarians should seize every opportunity to demonstrate the value libraries contribute. At the very least, users should know that the library is what got them there. In developing virtual environments that support access, it also is important to take into account the social environment within which users operate, because it influences their decisions to use and adopt different tools and technologies.

Build relationships based on trust

Ultimately, users want to be able to trust their virtual environment and its offerings. Trust can take on different meanings based on the situation of use. While Millennials may want assurances about who is monitoring virtual reference services (VRS) before deciding to use them, scholars sharing and reusing data through a digital repository may want assurances that the data are being preserved and the repository is sustainable. These are two very different kinds of assurances for two very different kinds of technologies and user groups. We all know the saying one size doesn't fit all. Librarians must put it into practice. Taking heed of the social dynamics at play in users' decisions to use and adopt technologies also must be part of the solution if libraries are to be successful.

Building a supportive library infrastructure has become more complicated. It's not just about the physical infrastructure anymore. We also must think about the technical one. Albeit different, we believe the two should be developed in coordination if they are to support common library goals. In addition, we must develop relationships that support ongoing dialogue with users in physical and virtual environments so they have expectations of and continued confidence and trust in evolving library offerings. Together, a well-integrated physical and technical infrastructure can provide added value to the library experience by creating an environment where users are able to access materials, engage with people and spaces and use equipment and technology.

Recommendations

As librarians continue to build infrastructure, it is important to build users' awareness of the changes as well as to maintain their trust. Although libraries enjoy a strong institutional reputation within the communities they serve, that doesn't necessarily translate into increased library usage. Research suggests ways users go about developing trust in online technologies and environments (Connaway and Dickey 2010; Connaway, Lanclos, and Hood 2013; Connaway, White et al. 2013; Van House 2002; Yakel et al., "Trust in Digital Repositories," 2013; Yoon 2013). Drawing from this work, we outline several recommendations for librarians to consider.

Provide a warm transfer

By working FtF with individuals, library staff can help increase trust on a personal level and can positively influence future library visits, both in-person and online, as approachability and genuine interest in the users' information needs can influence their engagement with library services (Connaway and Radford 2011). A way to leverage and extend the bond created between users and librarians in the physical environment is to demonstrate online systems and services during in-person encounters, such as by clicking through a database to demonstrate how to develop a query and to select sources (Connaway and Radford 2011). When it comes to VRS, this type of warm transfer is particularly important to younger individuals, some of whom have been taught to be wary of strangers who may lurk online (Connaway and Radford 2011).

Understand and internalize users' interests

Identification with people involves understanding and internalizing their interests (Lewicki and Bunker 1996). Research suggests identification plays a role in building trust in organizations and their technology (Pirson and Malhotra 2011; Sitkin and Roth 1993; Yakel et al., "Trust in Digital Repositories," 2013). But how does an organization demonstrate that it identifies with its users?

Walter and Mediavilla (2005) suggest having users participate in the development of library systems and services to feel that their needs and preferences are acknowledged and considered. We believe this idea can be applied beyond the initial development cycle. In an evaluation of a virtual research environment, Faniel (2009) suggests that changes to the technical infrastructure should be negotiated on an ongoing basis, and challenges should be recognized and reconciled during a process that is more inclusive of the users who the changes affect.

Libraries also can show a commitment to internalizing users' interests at the point of need. Librarians can think about installing pop-up chat services on library websites and in online catalogs when users are idle or their search retrieves no sources (Connaway and Radford 2011). Users suggest having librarians roam the library with mobile technology to see who might need their help (Prabha, Connaway, and Dickey 2006). The idea is to provide flexible, customizable systems and services that allow for feedback (Partridge and Hallam 2006). This includes not only identifying ownership of print and digital materials but also providing access to these materials.

Participants of a focus group in 2012 reiterated this when they stated that it's not worth users' time for a library system to identify ownership of print and digital materials that aren't readily available and accessible for use (Connaway and Wakeling 2012). Knowing that a library owns an item is of little value to them if the item is not accessible.

Demonstrate library value

A warm transfer might get library visitors to use online systems and services. However, it doesn't address those who currently are using online alternatives that are openly available on the Web. Some academic library users do not know what materials are offered by the library nor do they know the difference between library-provided databases and online journals and openly available sources on the Web (Connaway, Lanclos, and Hood 2013; Connaway, Lanclos et al. 2013; Prabha, Connaway, and Dickey 2006). The frequency with which this confusion occurs for undergraduates indicates the need for marketing the content available at and provided by the library and the importance of branding online library sources (Williams 2006).

Some college and university librarians provide video introductions to themselves on the library website or YouTube that are linked to the library website (Lippincott and Duckett 2013). This provides faces and names for individuals to connect with FtF or virtually. Librarians also may want to provide video instruction on how to improve discovery and access through the open Web and how to review search results and determine relevant and authoritative sources. Why not show users the best of both words by synthesizing search results from alternative information services, such as Google, with results from the library's discovery and access systems? This provides a way for librarians to honestly and effectively demonstrate the value the library brings to research, teaching and learning beyond the popular alternatives.

Toot your own horn

The value librarians create across a range of activities also must be made more visible so that librarians' expertise is identified and eventually internalized (Dempsey 2012). As librarians engage with the academic community, they can articulate their expertise and new library services. Faculty at the University of Houston expressed surprise that librarians could offer research data services beyond traditional library instruction (Peters and Dryden 2011). The authors concluded that their study of faculty behavior provided a tremendous opportunity for library outreach by meeting people where they work and socializing while delivering and promoting existing library services (Peters and Dryden 2011).

As library services continue to evolve, we recommend incorporating explicit promotion of librarians' expertise. "By putting librarians out there as faculty services specialists, we promote their role as academic partners and we advance the concept that 'building' and 'collections' are only parts of the array of information services that we can deliver" (Pritchard 2008, 229). It is imperative that librarians continually articulate the value of the academic library by demonstrating the degree to which the library contributes to institutional mission and goals (Association of College and Research Libraries 2010). This can include reporting the results of user-centered inquiry and the measurement of achievement, GPA, degree completion and retention rate based on student engagement with library services and resources. The goal is to educate the campus community that libraries and librarians should be a go-to source for information needs and services.

Leverage the power of social influence

Librarians should not dismiss the influence peers and mentors have on the initial use and adoption of library systems and services and should figure out ways to use it to the library's advantage. Students interact with friends, fellow students, lecturers, tutors and library staff, in addition to experts and professionals when seeking information (Connaway, Lanclos, and Hood 2013; Connaway and Radford 2011; Diehm and Lupton 2012), depending upon the context and situation of their needs. This means that librarians need to offer content, interaction and services in multiple environments and formats. The academic library needs to have a presence, both physically on campus and virtually through social media and a Web presence, which can be difficult with limited resources. People who didn't use VRS indicated that they would try it if it were recommended by a trusted librarian, colleague or friend (Connaway and Radford 2011). A similar phenomenon is at work for those seeking data to reuse. More experienced social scientists were found to point novices to data repositories and to influence their future data sharing and reuse behavior (Faniel, Kriesberg, and Yakel 2012; Kriesberg et al. 2013). Peers and colleagues also were found to influence trust in and use of repositories (Yakel et al., "Trust in Digital Repositories," 2013; Yoon 2013).

Conclusion

The accessibility of print materials still is important to many people. Despite an explosion of new formats and various delivery methods, printed books appear to have a secure future in libraries. People still want them and actively search for them, especially known titles. And while all-digital libraries are emerging, print collections in libraries still have a place and are likely to continue to have a place in the future. However, the library is not the first place people go for help with their personal and academic information needs. This should not be viewed as a failure but an opportunity. It's an opportunity for librarians to promote and develop new ways to engage, get to know and create relationships with their communities.

The opportunity starts with the recognition that "books are for use" encompasses more than the content that needs to be preserved and organized for access. The library Ranganathan knew has undergone dramatic changes in scope, mission and service models. Today, libraries must allow users to move between two worlds—the physical and the virtual. Like Ranganathan, we suggest the law "books are for use" look beyond the content to the infrastructure with a focus on issues related to access. However, in our view, the supportive infrastructure requires a focus on rethinking not only the physical but also the technical infrastructure associated with providing content.

The future use and usefulness of physical and digital library materials depends on more than people's demand for it. Libraries have to deliver. The future of library materials depends on the reliability and integrity of the infrastructure that provides access to them. Moreover, as users' needs and expectations shift, the materials and the infrastructure must shift in turn at the very least. Preempting the users' shift and meeting them there at their point of need would be even better. We know this is easier said than done, but we believe ongoing assessment and change of the physical and technical infrastructure is imperative to ensure continued effectiveness and use, and this should be carried out with an understanding of the social environment in which users inhabit.

References

American Libraries Editors. 2013. Manufacturing makerspaces. *American Library Association* (February 6), http://www.americanlibrariesmagazine.org/article/manufacturing-makerspaces.

Association of College and Research Libraries. 2010. *Value of academic libraries: A comprehensive research review and report.* Researched by Megan Oakleaf. Chicago: Association of College and Research Libraries. http://www.acrl.ala.org/value/.

Auckland, Mary. 2012. *Re-skilling for research.* London: Research Information Network. http://www.rluk.ac.uk/files/RLUK%20Re-skilling.pdf.

Barner, Keren. 2011. The library is a growing organism: Ranganathan's Fifth Law of library science and the academic library in the digital era. *Library Philosophy and Practice* (September), http://unllib.unl.edu/LPP/barner.htm.

Bhatt, R. K. 2011. Relevance of Ranganathan's Laws of Library Science in library marketing. *Library Philosophy and Practice* (July), http://unllib.unl.edu/LPP/bhatt.htm.

Calhoun, Karen, Joanne Cantrell, Peggy Gallagher, and Janet Hawk. 2009. *Online catalogs: What users and librarians want: An OCLC report.* Dublin, OH: OCLC.

Carlson, Jacob, Michael Fosmire, C. C. Miller, and Megan Sapp Nelson. 2011. Determining data information literacy needs: A study of students and research faculty. *portal: Libraries and the Academy* 11, no. 2: 629-57. http://muse.jhu.edu/journals/pla/summary/v011/11.2.carlson.html.

Carlson, Jake, Lisa Johnston, Brian Westra, and Mason Nichols. 2013. Developing an approach for data management education: A report from the data information literacy project. *The International Journal of Digital Curation* 8, no. 1: 204-217. http://www.ijdc.net/index.php/ijdc/article/view/254.

Carlson, Jake, and Marianne Stowell-Bracke. 2013. Data management and sharing from the perspective of graduate students: An examination of the culture and practice at the water quality field station. *portal: Libraries and the Academy* 13, no. 4: 343-61.

Carr, Patrick L. 2014. Reimagining the library as a technology: An analysis of Ranganathan's Five Laws of library science within the social construction of technology framework. *The Library Quarterly* 84, no. 2: 152-64.

Choudhury, G. Sayeed. 2008. Case study in data curation at John Hopkins University. *Library Trends* 57, no. 2: 211-20.

Choudury, Sayeed. 2010. Data curation: An ecological perspective. *College & Research Libraries News* 71: 194-96.

Cloonan, Michele V., and John G. Dove. 2005. Ranganathan online: Do digital libraries violate the Third Law? *Library Journal* 130, no. 6: 58-60.

Connaway, Lynn Silipigni, and Timothy J. Dickey. 2010. *The digital information seeker: Report of findings from selected OCLC, RIN, and JISC user behavior projects*. n.p.: Higher Education Funding Council for England (HEFCE). http://www.jisc.ac.uk/media/documents/publications/reports/2010/digitalinformationseekerreport.pdf.

Connaway, Lynn Silipigni, Timothy J. Dickey, and Marie L. Radford. 2011. "If it is too inconvenient I'm not going after it:" Convenience as a critical factor in information-seeking behaviors. *Library & Information Science Research* 33, no. 3: 179-90. http://www.oclc.org/content/dam/research/publications/library/2011/connaway-lisr.pdf.

Connaway, Lynn Silipigni, Donna Lanclos, and Erin M. Hood. 2013. "I find Google a lot easier than going to the library website." Imagine ways to innovate and inspire students to use the academic library. *Proceedings of the Association of College & Research Libraries (ACRL) 2013 conference, April 10-13, 2013, Indianapolis, IN*. Chicago: Association of College & Research Libraries. http://www.ala.org/acrl/sites/ala.org.acrl/files/content/conferences/confsandpreconfs/2013/papers/Connaway_Google.pdf.

Connaway, Lynn Silipigni, Donna Lanclos, David White, Alison Le Cornu, and Erin M. Hood. 2013. User-centered decision making: A new model for developing academic library services and systems. *IFLA Journal* 39, no. 1: 30-36.

Connaway, Lynn Silipigni, Chandra Prabha, and Timothy J. Dickey. 2006. *Sense-making the information confluence: The whys and hows of college and university user satisficing of information needs. Phase III: Focus group interview study.* Report on National Leadership Grant LG-02-03-0062-03, to Institute of Museum and Library Services, Washington, DC. Columbus, OH: School of Communication, The Ohio State University.

Connaway, Lynn Silipigni, and Marie L. Radford. 2011. *Seeking synchronicity: Revelations and recommendations for virtual reference.* Dublin, OH: OCLC Research. http://www.oclc.org/reports/synchronicity/full.pdf.

Connaway, Lynn Silipigni, and Simon Wakeling. 2012. *To use or not to use WorldCat.org: An international perspective from different user groups.* Unpublished report, April 26.

Connaway, Lynn Silipigni, David White, Donna Lanclos, and Alison Le Cornu. 2013. Visitors and Residents: What motivates engagement with the digital information environment? *Information Research* 18, no. 1, http://informationr.net/ir/18-1/infres181.html.

Cragin, Melissa H., Carole L. Palmer, Jacob R. Carlson, and Michael Witt. 2010. Data sharing, small science and institutional repositories. *Philosophical Transactions of the Royal Society* 368, no. 1926: 4023-4038. http://rsta.royalsocietypublishing.org/content/368/1926.toc.

Daniels, Morgan, Ixchel Faniel, Kathleen Fear, and Elizabeth Yakel. 2012. Managing fixity and fluidity in data repositories. In *iConference 2012, February 7-10, 2012, Toronto, ON, Canada,* 279-286. New York: ACM.

Dasgupta, Arjun. 2007. "Library staff" and Ranganathan's Five Laws. *IASLIC Bulletin* 52, no. 4: 195-204.

De Rosa, Cathy, Joanne Cantrell, Matthew Carlson, Peggy Gallagher, Janet Hawk, and Charlotte Sturtz. 2010. *Perceptions of libraries, 2010: Context and community.* Dublin, OH: OCLC Online Computer Library Center.

De Rosa, Cathy, Joanne Cantrell, Diane Cellentani, Janet Hawk, Lillie Jenkins, and Alane Wilson. 2005. *Perceptions of libraries and information resources: A report to the OCLC Membership.* Dublin, OH: OCLC Online Computer Library Center.

Delserone, Leslie M. 2008. At the watershed: Preparing for research data management and stewardship at the University of Minnesota Libraries. *Library Trends* 57, no. 2: 202-210.

Dempsey, Lorcan. 2012. Thirteen ways of looking at libraries, discovery, and the catalog: Scale, workflow, attention. *EDUCAUSE Review Online* (December 10), http://www.educause.edu/ero/article/thirteen-ways-looking-libraries-discovery-and-catalog-scale-workflow-attention.

Diehm, Rae-Anne, and Mandy Lupton. 2012. Approaches to learning information literacy: A phenomenographic study. *The Journal of Academic Librarianship* 38, no. 5: 217-25.

EDUCAUSE Learning Initiative. 2013. 7 things you should know about makerspaces. *EDUCAUSE* (April 9), http://www.educause.edu/library/resources/7-things-you-should-know-about-makerspaces.

Faniel, Ixchel M. 2009. *Unrealized potential: The socio-technical challenges of a large scale cyberinfrastructure initiative.* Arlington, VA: National Science Foundation. http://hdl.handle.net/2027.42/61845.

Faniel, Ixchel, Lynn Silipigni Connaway, and Kendra Parson. 2014. 20th Annual Reference Research Forum. Presented at ALA Annual Conference & Exhibition, June 26-July 1, in Las Vegas, NV.

Faniel, Ixchel M., and Trond E. Jacobsen. 2010. Reusing scientific data: How earthquake engineering researchers assess the reusability of colleagues' data. *Computer Supported Cooperative Work* 19, no. 3-4: 355-75.

Faniel, Ixchel, Eric Kansa, Sarah Whitcher Kansa, Julianna Barrera-Gomez, and Elizabeth Yakel. 2013. The challenges of digging data: A study of context in archaeological data reuse. In *JCDL 2013 Proceedings of the 13th ACM/IEEE-CS Joint Conference on Digital Libraries*, 295-304. New York: ACM. http://dx.doi.org/10.1145/2467696.2467712.

Faniel, Ixchel M., Adam Kriesberg, and Elizabeth Yakel. 2012. Data reuse and sensemaking among novice social scientists. Paper presented at the annual meeting of the American Society for Information Science and Technology, October 26-31, in Baltimore, Maryland.

Fisher, Erin. 2012. Makerspaces move into academic libraries. *ACRL TechConnect* (November 28), http://acrl.ala.org/techconnect/?p=2340.

Glassmeyer, Sarah. 2010. Ranganathan 2.0. *AALL Spectrum* 14, no. 3: 22-24.

Goldup, Stacey Jeanette. 2010. *Public libraries in the digital age: Investing the implementation of Ranganathan's Five Laws of library science in physical and online library services.* Report submitted to the School of Information Management, Victoria University of Wellington, February 2010.

Gorman, Michael. 1995. Five new laws of librarianship. *American Libraries* 26, no. 8: 784-85.

Gorman, Michael. 1998. The five laws of library science: Then & now. Excerpt of *Our singular strengths*, by Michael Gorman. *School Library Journal* 7: 20-23.

Hiebert, Jean, and Shelly Theriault. 2012. BLASTing the zombies! Creative ideas to fight finals fatigue. *College & Research Libraries News* 73, no. 9: 540-69.

Jahnke, Lori, Andrew Asher, and Spencer D. C. Keralis. 2012. *The problem of data.* With an introduction by Charles Henry. Washington, DC: Council on Library and Information Resources.

Johnston, Lisa, and Cody Hanson. 2010. e-Science at the University of Minnesota: A collaborative approach. *International Association of Scientific and Technological University Libraries, 31st Annual Conference,* http://docs.lib.purdue.edu/iatul2010/conf/day2/3.

Johnston, Lisa, and Jon Jeffryes. 2013. Data management skills needed by structural engineering students: Case study at the University of Minnesota. *Journal of Professional Issues in Engineering Education and Practice* 140, no. 2, http://dx.doi.org/10.1061/(ASCE)EI.1943-5541.0000154.

Kriesberg, Adam, Rebecca D. Frank, Ixchel M. Faniel, and Elizabeth Yakel. 2013. The role of data reuse in the apprenticeship process. *ASIST 2013, November 1-6, 2013, Montreal, Quebec, Canada.*

Kwanya, Tom, Christine Stilwell, and Peter G. Underwood. 2010. Library 2.0 principles and Ranganathan's Fifth Law. *Mousaion* 28, no. 2: 1-16.

Lewicki, Roy J., and Barbara Benedict Bunker. 1996. Developing and maintaining trust in work relationships. In *Trust in organizations: Frontiers of theory and research*, edited by Roderick Kramer and Tom Tyler, 114-39. Thousand Oaks, CA: Sage Publications.

Lippincott, Joan K. 2010. A mobile future for academic libraries. *Reference Services Review* 38, no. 2: 205-213.

Lippincott, Joan K., and Kim Duckett. 2013. Library space assessment: Focusing on learning. *Research Library Issues: A Report from ARL, CNI, and SPARC* 284: 12-21. http://publications.arl.org/rli284/.

Nelson, Bryn. 2009. Data sharing: Empty archives. *Nature* 461, no. 7261: 160–63. http://www.nature.com/news/2009/090909/pdf/461160a.pdf.

Newton, Mark P., C. C. Miller, and Marianne S. Bracke. 2010. Librarian roles in institutional repository data set collecting: Outcomes of a research library task force. *Collection Management* 36, no. 1: 53-67. Doi: 10.1080/01462679.2011.530546.

Noruzi, Alireza. 2004. Application of Ranganathan's Laws to the web. *Webology* 1, no. 2, http://www.webology.org/2004/v1n2/a8.html.

Odum Library. Odum library makerspace. Valdosta State University. https://www.valdosta.edu/academics/library/depts/circulation/makerspace.php.

Partridge, Helen, and Gillian Hallam. 2006. Educating the Millennial generation for evidence based information practice. *Library Hi Tech* 24, no. 3: 400-419. http://www.emeraldinsight.com/journals.htm?articleid=1571818&.

Peters, Christie, and Anita Riley Dryden. 2011. Assessing the academic library's role in campus-wide research data management: A first step at the University of Houston. *Science & Technology Libraries* 30, no. 4: 387-403. http://www.tandfonline.com/doi/pdf/10.1080/0194262X.2011.626340.

Pierard, Cindy, and Norice Lee. 2011. Studying space: Improving space planning with user studies. *Journal of Access Services* 8: 190-207. Doi: 10.1080/15367967.2011.602258.

Pirson, Michael, and Deepak Malhotra. 2011. Foundations of organizational trust: What matters to different stakeholders? *Organization Science* 22, no. 4: 1087-1104. http://pubsonline.informs.org/doi/abs/10.1287/orsc.1100.0581.

Prabha, Chandra, Lynn Silipigni Connaway, and Timothy J. Dickey. 2006. *Sense-making the information confluence: The whys and hows of college and university user satisficing of information needs. Phase IV: Semi-structured interview study.* Report on National Leadership Grant LG-02-03-0062-03, to Institute of Museum and Library Services, Washington, DC. Columbus, OH: School of Communication, The Ohio State University.

Prieto, Adolfo G. 2009. From conceptual to perceptual reality: Trust in digital repositories. *Library Review* 58, no. 8: 593-606. http://www.emeraldinsight.com/journals.htm?issn=0024-2535.

Pritchard, Sarah M. 2008. Deconstructing the library: Reconceptualizing collections, spaces and services. *Journal of Administration* 48, no. 2: 219-33. http://www.tandfonline.com/doi/abs/10.1080/01930820802231492#.U3OLI_ldVMg.

Ranganathan, Shiyali Ramamrita. 1931. *The five laws of library science.* London: Edward Goldston, Ltd.

Research Information Network. 2006. *Researchers and discovery services: Behaviour, perceptions and needs.* London: Research Information Network.

Research Information Network. 2008. *To share or not to share: Publication and quality assurance of research data outputs.* London: Research Information Network.

Ross, Seamus, and Andrew McHugh. 2006. The role of evidence in establishing trust in repositories. *D-Lib Magazine* 12, no. 7/8, http://www.dlib.org/dlib/july06/ross/07ross.html.

Sadler, Shawna. 2012. Session 3: Exploiting space as a distinctive asset. Presented at Libraries rebound: Embracing mission, maximizing impact, June 5-6, in Philadelphia, PA. https://www.youtube.com/watch?v=AmEtdVPro54&feature=youtu.be.

Salo, Dorothea. 2008. Innkeeper at the roach motel. *Library Trends* 57, no. 2: 98-123.

Sayogo, Djoko Sigit, and Theresa A. Pardo. 2012. Exploring the motive for data publication in open data initiative: Linking intention to action. *2012 45th Hawaii International Conference on System Sciences.*

Sitkin, Sim B., and Nancy L. Roth. 1993. Explaining the limited effectiveness of legalistic "remedies" for trust/distrust. *Organizational Science* 4: 367–92. http://www.jstor.org/stable/2634950.

Soehner, Catherine, Catherine Steeves, and Jennifer Ward. 2010. *e-Science and data support services: A study of ARL member institutions,* http://www.arl.org/bm~doc/escience_report2010.pdf.

Tenopir, Carol, Suzie Allard, Kimberly Douglass, Arsev Umur Aydinoglu, Lei Wu, Eleanor Read, Maribeth Manoff, and Mike Frame. 2011. Data sharing by scientists: Practices and perceptions. *PLoS ONE* 6, no. 6: e21101. http://www.plosone.org/article/info%3Adoi%2F10.1371%2Fjournal.pone.0021101.

Tenopir, Carol, Ben Birch, and Suzie Allard. 2012. *Academic libraries and research data services: Current practices and plans for the future. An ACRL white paper.* Chicago: Association of College and Research Libraries.

Van House, Nancy. 2002. Digital libraries and practices of trust: Networked biodiversity information. *Social Epistemology: A Journal of Knowledge, Culture and Policy* 16, no. 1: 99. Doi: 10.1080/02691720210132833.

Van House, Nancy A., Mark H. Butler, and Lisa R. Schiff. 1998. Cooperative knowledge work and practices of trust: Sharing environmental planning data sets. In *Proceedings of the 1998 ACM Conference On Computer Supported Cooperative Work*, 335–43. Seattle, WA: ACM. Doi:10.1145/289444.289508.

Walter, Scott. 2012. Ranganathan redux: The "Five Laws" and the future of college & research libraries. *College & Research Libraries* 73, no. 3: 213-15.

Walter, Virginia A., and Cindy Mediavilla. 2005. Teens are from Neptune, librarians are from Pluto: An analysis of online reference transactions. *Library Trends* 54, no. 2: 209–227.

Watters, Audrey. 2013. The case for campus makerspace. *Hack Education* (February 6), http://hackeducation.com/2013/02/06/the-case-for-a-campus-makerspace/.

Williams, Lesley. 2006. Making "e" visible. *Library Journal* 13, no. 11: 40-43.

Witt, Michael. 2008. Institutional repositories and research data curation in a distributed environment. *Library Trends* 57, no. 2:191-201.

Yakel, Elizabeth, Ixchel Faniel, Adam Kriesberg, and Ayoung Yoon. 2013. Trust in digital repositories. *The International Journal of Digital Curation* 8, no. 1, http://www.ijdc.net/index.php/ijdc/article/view/8.1.143/303.

Yoon, Ayoung. 2013. End users' trust in data repositories: Definition and influences on trust development. *Archival Science* 14, no. 1: 17-34. Doi: 10.1007/s10502-013-9207-8.

Zickuhr, Kathryn, Lee Rainie, and Kristen Purcell. 2013. *Library services in the digital age.* Washington, DC: Pew Research Center's Internet & American Life Project. http://libraries.pewinternet.org/files/legacy-pdf/PIP_Library%20services_Report.pdf.

4

Every book its reader.

> **"** It is doubtful whether open-access can achieve all that it can for the Third Law if the library staff interpret open-access to mean 'Provide the books and keep out of the way of the readers as much as possible...' It is doubtful whether the card catalogue, by itself, will ever become the guide, philosopher and friend of the ordinary reader of a library... The mechanical organization of a library—however desirable—can never be carried to the point of dispensing with personal service. The requirement of the Third Law defies and transcends machinery. It will always require the provision of human beings as 'canvassing agents' for books."
> **—Ranganathan 1931, 312-13**

The new fourth law: Every book its reader

The cynical way to achieve "every book its reader," Ranganathan (1931) noted, is to have as few books as possible, drastically decreasing the numerator in the books per reader equation. In previous centuries, the whole purpose of literacy in some cultures was to master a small, specific canon of religious texts. In those circumstances, "every book its reader" would have been an easy task for a librarian. Few books, few readers. Problem solved.

A cynical interpretation of this law, however, may not require nearly as much time traveling to encounter. Tired of defending his preferred genre of literature—science fiction—against charges of inferiority based on its worst examples, author and critic Theodore Sturgeon made the now-famous observation (later termed "Sturgeon's Law") that "ninety percent of everything is crud" (Wikipedia contributors 2014).

We are all, of course, familiar with arguments from various authorities that disparage particular works, authors, genres or entire types of media. Claims of quality have come and gone throughout history as yesterday's scandalous, trivial novel has become today's required reading for literature students.

The best (or most entertaining) counter to the idea of limiting the amount of content that's valuable for study, analysis or use may come from a corollary written on TV Tropes, a wiki site dedicated to examining and cataloging "tricks of the trade for writing fiction" (TV Tropes contributors):

> TV Tropes Corollary: The difficulty of getting a group of people to agree on which 10% is not crud exponentially approaches infinity as the size of the group increases. (TV Tropes contributors)

If you object to the use of a quote from a wiki about writing for TV in a scholarly report such as this, we would respectfully suggest that you have just proved its veracity, thus justifying its use.

This sentiment fits beautifully, of course, within the laws as Ranganathan intended them. "Every book its reader" depends entirely on the previous law "every person his or her book." While libraries always have had to make collection development choices based on both budgets and the needs, or perceived needs, of the communities they serve, doing so from a judgmental, restrictive stance has rarely been well received in the long run.

Moreover, now that we have opened up the definition of what "book" means to include any possible medium, including raw data and transactional information of all kinds, we're left with the inescapable conclusion that "every book" means, essentially, every single, possible piece of communicative material that anyone, anywhere might find useful. Because as the population you serve increases, agreement on which 10% is not crud exponentially approaches infinity.

Librarians no longer are legitimately able to say, "we don't cover that topic" or "we can't help you with that question." In the connected, link-centric world of the Web, there are always sources, and there are always answers. Anyone a library turns away will seek answers elsewhere, often satisficing and taking sources that may not be authoritative.

To address these changes, our recommendations at the end of this chapter will take the points Ranganathan made when expounding on this law and will derive three values that are broadly applicable today:

- Discoverability
- Access
- Use

and, above all else, librarians themselves, the "canvassing agents" providing personal service in order to help maximize all of the above.

In his book, *Everything Bad is Good for You*, author Stephen Johnson (2005, 11–12) makes the point that for popular culture, "certain kinds of environments encourage cognitive complexity... the cultural object—the film or video game—is not a metaphor for that system; it's more like an output or a result." He goes on to say that "to understand these forces we'll need to draw upon disciplines that don't usually interact with one another: economics, narrative theory, social network analysis, neuroscience" (Johnson 2005, 11). Johnson is attempting to get at something he calls "The Sleeper Curve," from the Woody Allen movie, *Sleeper*, in which scientists from the future find great cultural (and even nutritional) worth in things that 20th century citizens derided as garbage.

Johnson is attempting to go beyond a qualitative, Sturgeon-esque evaluation of which materials are not crud. He is trying to quantify the other 90% as being worthy of study simply because they represent the output or a result of our culture, which is important and educational in certain contexts.

Or, as Rene Belloq, the villain in *Raiders of the Lost Ark*, put it:

> Look at this. [holds up a silver pocket watch] It's worthless. Ten dollars from a vendor in the street. But I take it, I bury it in the sand for a thousand years, it becomes priceless! (*Raiders of the Lost Ark*, 1981)

We don't know what materials may be important to a particular student, researcher, author or community. We can't, as Ranganathan said, cynically reduce the content we make available in order to simplify the job of librarian. We know that:

- Every book has a reader;

- Every TV show has its fans (and critics);

- Every piece of data is useful to some researcher;

- Every emoticon is important to a teen (or cultural historian); and

- Every pocket watch will be treasured, some day, by an archaeologist.

What we can do is apply modern tools and programs to Ranganathan's third law, our fourth, to help connect them as efficiently and elegantly as possible.

Examining the law in today's environment

It is difficult to determine how best to get relevant and authoritative content into the hands of users. We know that preferred media change over time, that access points evolve and that social and cultural environments differ greatly from person to person. Librarians today are faced with the challenge of developing and updating collections and services to meet the needs of multiple generations of users with differing approaches to information seeking (Connaway et al. 2008). Every book may have its reader, but the path from book to reader is going to differ greatly based on a variety of factors.

> " The mission of the librarian is to build a well-organized collection of resources in order to maximize the chance that users will find what they need. The third law is also subtle. 'Every book, its reader' almost means that 'resources look for people'. Thus, the job of librarians is to help these resources find the people who want and need them the most. Library patrons, Ranganathan points out, often do not know enough about available resources to know what to request. Any organization of the electronic or physical library that focuses only on getting the readers what they ask for neglects two key components of good library practice: browsing and linking."
> —**Cloonan and Dove 2005, 58**

Across a variety of research, however, we see three broad trends in the attempt to understand and address information-seeking behavior with regards to connecting "every book" to its reader:

- Understanding the flow in workflow;

- Acknowledging the role of online social interaction; and

- Paying more attention to context.

In any environment, making connections will depend, to a large degree, on understanding the environment itself as opposed to any individual points of reference. These three areas hold the potential to help provide a framework on which we then can move forward to make our interpretations and recommendations.

User workflows—connecting the dots

Addressing the learning goals of the communities they serve has been at the heart of library management and collection building from the beginning. What has changed more rapidly in recent decades, though, are the tools with which these communities address their own needs. This is especially true when compared to the speed that librarians are willing and able to change alongside their users.

When examining the landscape, some tools are clearly more universal. For example, many information seekers, regardless of demographics, tend to demonstrate heavy use of Web information sources, such as Wikipedia and Google (Connaway and Dickey 2010; Connaway, Prabha, and Dickey 2006; Head and Eisenberg 2010; Prabha, Connaway, and Dickey 2006). On the other hand, college students rate libraries significantly higher than all respondents in terms of lifestyle fit, for both online and for physical libraries (De Rosa et al. 2006). And journal articles are reported as the main resource of interest to researchers (Research Information Network 2006).

These specific insights are helpful, of course. But they also are fairly consistent with any common-sense evaluation of information-seeking behaviors:

- A more general-purpose tool, such as Google, is going to be more widely relied upon across a variety of groups;

- College students, whose campus lives are in close proximity to a library and who are called upon to do regular research, will rely more heavily on library resources both because of convenience and necessity;

- Researchers, whose stock-in-trade is journal articles, will most likely need access to those materials more than other audiences.

With regard to the law of matching every book to its reader, however, these issues provide points within a workflow, not examples of actual workflows. How so?

- Google is the how of the search, not the what. Search engines are, by design, not sticky sources of information but slippery portals to other sites.

- While college students are inclined to rely more heavily on the library, the library is the who of their flow, not the what or the how. Are they using the library for high-speed wifi access? For meeting and social space? For access to print materials?

- Researchers value journal articles, yes. But the articles are the what. But how do they find them?

Any information workflow relies on some combination of these elements, of course. To add value, we should understand the relationships between them and how they're changing. The distance between any information need and the right book always is at least two points. The difference between a successful, efficient workflow and one with dissatisfying results lies in the length and frustration caused by that distance.

> "…researchers with the most experience (20 years or more) seem in general to make less use than their less experienced colleagues of most categories of discovery services, and the less experienced are more likely to use most categories of service…There is no single, immediately apparent reason for less experienced researchers to be more intensive users: it is possible that it arises from the lack of formal training available to researchers: they may not be acting as sophisticated searchers and are perhaps fearful of missing significant information. This concern is found among many researchers."
> —Research Information Network 2006, 39

Improving and enhancing the workflow experience for users is essential to how libraries interact with their communities. Libraries are rarely the determiner of information needs or the source of materials themselves. They are perceived as mediators, helping to bridge the gap by connecting the dots between user requirements and available resources. The term disintermediation has been used to broadly describe how libraries have been affected by the Internet revolution. Whereas many materials used to be available only through libraries, now users can find them directly online, often from multiple sources. So, not only are there more dots, but users can connect them on their own as part of their workflow, which may or may not lead to library materials.

> 66
>
> The library cannot expect its users to build their workflow around the library; it must reach out into the workflows its users are creating on the network."
> —**Dempsey 2008**

What is required in many cases now are new kinds of mediation that support discovery, access and use. Archives, libraries and cultural heritage institutions have used social networking technologies such as Facebook, Twitter and blogs with some success. The library at the University of Nevada, Reno brought their special collections to life by creating pages for several students who attended the university in the early 1900s. They used the individuals' daily activities to promote the collection. It resulted in millions of Facebook friends for the students highlighted in the entries and an increase in use of the collections (DeSantis 2012). However, the issue is that the library's Facebook pages, Twitter streams and blog posts are not part of the users' workflow in the same way as Google or Wikipedia (Connaway, Lanclos, and Hood 2013a, 2013b). Several academic libraries have increased discovery of their collections by adding links to Wikipedia (Elder, Westrbook, and Reilly 2012; Lally and Dunford 2007; Szajewski 2013).

One year after linking 40 digital assets from the Hague Sheet Music Collection, Szajewski (2013) reported, "The number of pageviews via Wikipedia during the one-year period after these assets were linked is 5.39 times greater than the total number of pageviews via any source for these assets for the one year prior to linking." Lally (2009) also reported the increase in Wikipedia traffic as an indication that "we are indeed somewhat more embedded in the information flow." The increases may be attributed to not only drawing in new audiences but also to shortening the path that connects existing audiences to the resources. The short story is to create options that allow users to craft personal workflows that are flexible and efficient for how they want to work.

Social connections—the oldest dots, newly permanent

The role of social networking and social media in information seeking has been studied at great length during the past decade.

> " We're all authors now because everyone's got a Facebook status to update and a Twitter feed. So there's an extraordinary explosion of content and communication so it makes it challenging to be found – but if you can be found, it makes it possible for these explosions to happen. Publishers are competing in a very noisy world where it's not just the media creating noise, but readers themselves are creating a lot of noise."
> —Greenfield 2012

This phenomenon and its activities—posting, commenting, sharing, liking, friending, reviewing, listing, up-voting, etc.—is interesting in part because of the volume. Seeing that a YouTube video sent to a friend last week via email now has 4 million more views makes one feel like a part of its success in a way that wasn't possible in the past. But we're also interested because these traces of social behavior are both expressible and quantifiable in very granular ways.

To be clear, we've always been social about our learning. Dervin, Reinhard, Kerr, Song, and Shen (2006) make the case that both faculty and students tend to turn toward peers in terms of information-seeking behavior. We have found the same trend in our studies of user behavior: faculty turns to co-workers and colleagues; graduate students turn to peers, instructors, and advisors; undergraduates to their friends and peers (Connaway and Dickey 2010; Connaway, Lanclos, and Hood 2013a, 2013b; Dervin et al. 2006; Faniel, Kriesberg, and Yakel 2012; Kriesberg et al. 2013; Yakel et al., "Trust in Digital Repositories," 2013).

This is not new. Seeing as convenience is known as the most significant factor in choosing among information sources, the most natural first step for information seeking is to ask the people with whom you're already in contact (Radford and Connaway 2008). Your contacts have a similar context, understand your vocabulary, have a vested, social interest in helping you and may, in fact, have asked similar questions in the past. It's so obvious that it is often neglected in terms of library resources. Librarians should ask themselves this question: when asked to find or recommend a resource, is your first inclination to begin digging yourself, using all the information-seeking tools developed as part of your training as a librarian? Or do you think to ask how you might, instead, help your user get in touch with peers who might have done similar tasks in the past?

The tendency to trust peers and peer-based evaluations of information sources is so strong that search giants such as Google have recently adjusted their rankings based on social interactions such as Facebook likes and Twitter posts. People want to know what their peers value, because in many cases, their peers are the ones who determine their success.

And while social connections always have been important in our lives, online social media and networking activities differ from traditional interactions in one important way: they leave more permanent marks (think of Amazon reviews vs. simply asking your friends for a recommendation for a good book). The former is available for wider dissemination, can be used (essentially) forever and can be merged with other ratings to provide an average score.

Online, social interactions are another set of important dots that information seekers will use to connect to what they need.

Complex contexts—connecting the right dots

In the article "Intellectual Access—It Takes More Than Accessibility," Kent Anderson draws from Maria Popova's distinction between access and accessibility to make the following observation:

> ...what OA [Open Access] advocates call 'access' is better termed 'accessibility'—meaning information can be accessed at no direct cost to the user. Despite accessibility, the information remains inaccessible in any functional sense—they can't apply it, understand it competently, or put it into context. The information is accessible, but the person has no access to its real value. (Anderson 2012)

Anderson points out a major issue in modern, Web-enabled information seeking that is highly relevant to the "every book its reader" law. When there is a profusion of resources and information services available, some of them will be, for whatever reason, wrong for a particular information seeker. The concern is whether the information seeker has enough experience and context to make that determination.

This is not an attempt to go back to Sturgeon's Law and argue that librarians should become the arbiters of which 10% of any content pile is good and worthy of users' attention. Any resource ("every book") may have value at some point in time to some particular user ("its reader"). What's important is providing the context in order for users to make those decisions given a rich and complicated information environment. We've seen recent evidence of this in the academic community in which researchers are increasingly reusing each other's data (Carlson and Anderson 2007; Faniel and Jacobsen 2010; Faniel et al. 2013; Faniel, Kriesberg, and Yakel 2012; Rolland and Lee 2013; Zimmerman 2008).

This relates both to workflow and social networking. In the absence of providing adequate context within information seekers' workflows to enable decision making, they fall back on what is already in place, which today often means social networking. They use colleagues, peers, advisors, friends, family. As discussed earlier, these relationships are important because they are perceived as being experienced and trusted.

As information professionals, then librarians need to provide services that not only connect more dots but also make access to deeper, more authoritative sources of context available in ways that users can adopt into their workflows. Connaway and Dickey (2010) suggest that online library catalogs should operate more like search engines, but that is only part of the story. "...The poor usability, high complexity, and lack of integration of many electronic resource discovery systems have raised the...barrier to information search and retrieval [and] distracts users from focusing on the content, analysis and evaluation that would help them learn and make sense of what they have discovered" (Wong et al. 2009, 5). However, Wong and colleagues also conclude "being able to operate a search engine does not mean that one is able to find the good quality information necessary to help us learn and to advance our society" (Wong et al. 2009, 5).

Users can't necessarily discern whether the content that rises to the top of a search engine result is relevant and trustworthy enough to meet the needs of their circumstances. Here, libraries are at an advantage with their staff acting as what Ranganathan (1931, 313) called "canvassing agents." Their ability to select credible materials and to help discern which content is best given a particular user's needs is missing from the search engine equation. Popova (2011) explains the role of digital archivists and content curators in this way:

> ...digital archivists solve the barrier of accessibility, by making content previously tucked away in analog archives available to the world wide web, and content curators solve the barrier of awareness, by bringing to our (limited) attention noteworthy pieces of information from these digitized archives and, ideally, contextualizing them within our existing framework of knowledge and interests. (Popova 2011)

Information professionals are excellent at helping connect the right dots between users' requirements and available resources. But in their absence and in the absence of library systems with low barriers to entry, users will rely on other ways to satisfy their needs, ways that may provide more, but not necessarily better, results.

Our interpretation of the law

As we said at the onset, our interpretation of Ranganathan's third law goes back to three areas that help connect "every book" to "its reader":

Increase the discoverability, access and use of resources within users' existing workflows.

An example of how all these factors come together in the context of workflow, social connections and context is drawn from a study of data reuse within the earthquake engineering (EE) community.

> " Our analysis of the data practices of EE researchers… strongly indicates… unique factors and judgments influence decisions to reuse colleagues' data, factors and judgments that cannot be satisfied merely by making more data more easily available. Before they are willing to reuse data created by others, EE researchers make judgments about the data's relevance, they seek confidence that potentially relevant data can be understood, and they must trust the data. To make these judgments, EE researchers use varied combinations of strategies, context information, and resources, in ways that have important implications for the continued development of the NEES [George E. Brown, Jr. Network for Earthquake Engineering Simulation] data repository and associated infrastructure."
> —**Faniel and Jacobsen 2010, 373**

Similar results have been found in other studies of discovery, access and use of various types of content (Barry 1994; Faniel, Kriesberg, and Yakel 2012; Faniel, Kansa, Kansa, Barrera-Gomez, and Yakel 2013; Rieh 2002; Wang and Soergel 1998). All three goals of this law—discoverability, access and use—are wrapped up in issues of workflow, social connections and context. Understanding not only what context people need but also how they get it and what they use it for will be important in determining how to best support them.

- First, users must be able to find relevant information—the discovery process, which is attached to workflow and social connections;

- Next, they must be able to get to it—accessibility, which is often a factor of both workflow and context; and

- Lastly, they must understand and trust it enough be able to decide to use it and have ways of doing so that are convenient and consistent with their goals. Here workflow, context and social connections come into play.

Notice workflow appears across all three goals. The same held true in Ranganathan's time. The main considerations for these three goals could be carried out, largely, within specific workflows. The examples he gives—reference works, shelf arrangement, open departments, catalog entries— are all found within the scope of the library itself, however. Librarians can do the work necessary to determine which reference works are most appropriate. They can improve shelf arrangements and other issues related to the physical library. They can make more resources accessible by digitizing rare materials, subscribing to more databases and journals, adding content and making resources more easily discoverable. They can improve the online library catalog experience to make it more like Google.

These all are important tasks, and they all improve discoverability, access and use. But they do so within the library's and not the users' workflows. Even taken at the level of the profession, these improvements tend to stop at the library's door or the online library catalog. Simply making a catalog look and behave more like Google won't ever make it as popular as Google. Improving the shelving to the point where it's as attractive and useful as any retail store display won't get the resources in front of users. And the largest set of journals is worthless if a researcher's peers are liking, Tweeting and linking elsewhere.

There are other factors identified in the literature regarding the importance understanding users' workflows (Prabha, Connaway, and Dickey 2006).

- The specific situation motivating the search influences the choice of sources. This is a clear indication of the need for motion portraits to describe user search strategies.

- Users make rational decisions, which are contextually based, as they carry out their information searches.

- Users choose a search strategy and a level of effort based on their situational needs, and they differentiate between quick and thorough searches

The place where most workflows—including social ones—begin and end is the Internet. "Every book its reader." It's such a simple phrase, but there are now trillions of pieces of information available, often in multiple, overlapping and contradictory usages (Spencer 2012). And every user is no longer just a reader, but a judge, reviewer, channel, content creator and, often, even a librarian. There are signs that libraries have begun to adapt to a flood of new workflows and are finding new ways to support this law, ways that adhere both to its original intent as well as new ones given the new environment.

Recommendations

For the three areas we've discussed throughout this chapter—discoverability, access, use—we have some specific thoughts about how to apply our interpretation.

Increase discovery through partnerships

In the case of our interpretation of this law, the path from "every book" to "its reader" is going to pass through a growing number of services, audiences, events and places. A piece of content may originate with a writer whose workflow exposes early drafts, thoughts and outlines in a form that is discoverable much earlier in the creative process, such as a blog. A researcher may not only publish in a journal but also may give a TED talk on the subject during the investigation phase. A publisher may provide several versions of a work, or content related to a work, in order to make it discoverable in different media, for example, the growing number of popular books that are released with video trailers on YouTube. And any of these also may be discussed and shared in social media.

These are examples of content creators and providers thinking laterally about how their materials can reach wider and more connected audiences. It's no longer enough to think writer to publisher to book store (or library) to reader. More dots to connect doesn't just refer to more original content; it refers to the points at which that content can intersect with users' preferred workflows.

Librarians are good at establishing partnerships within the communities they serve, whether that means faculty and students at a university or citizens within a geographic area. Establishing partnerships further afield, however, can be tricky. This is not to say that librarians don't work well with others. They work especially well with other librarians for services, such as interlibrary loan, whose scope predates many retail industries' ability to service widely dispersed customers. The ability of a student in Quebec to be able to access materials in Mexico City well before the arrival of the Internet is a testament to the power of library cooperation.

To become discoverable in more workflows, librarians must apply that same philosophy to partnerships outside the "normal" scope of librarianship. This might manifest as:

- Working with technology companies to expose library metadata into more and vastly different user workflows;

- Teaming with logistics companies to solve issues of shared print collections, such as transportation and delivery of physical materials;

- Reaching out through academic communities to the professional organizations and industries that serve and are served by them in order to understand their challenges;

- Making library data compatible with other formats, such as linked data; and

- Offering library resources—whether expertise, bandwidth, physical space or networking opportunities—to business leaders.

This is not necessarily a comfortable activity, and there will be false starts. But as long as libraries rely heavily on users coming to library-specific places, "every book" will have many fewer ways to be discovered by "its reader."

Increase access through redundancy

Access should never be singular. Having materials in one format may not be enough when serving users with widely diverse needs and workflows. Again, in terms of traditional library relationships and requirements, there have been many efforts along these lines. Libraries are often one of the only places in town or on campus where information seekers with barriers to accessibility can get to relevant materials in a variety of formats.

> " Participants also desire more digitized sources of all kinds, including digitization of older literature, sheet music, and art images. This finding is especially interesting because library digitization efforts to date have tended to center on materials in the sciences and social sciences; the study participants, though encompassing a broad disciplinary range, speak of digitization gaps principally in humanities collections."
> —**Connaway, Prabha, and Dickey 2006, 20**

But today, the concern for libraries isn't just whether the material can be accessed but whether it will be (Popova 2011). The fact that a book, map or video exists and is available for physical checkout in the library doesn't mean that it will be highly valued as an information source by audiences who have many other options.

When approaching a particular set of materials or services, librarians must ask themselves, "How can this be leveraged such that we can deliver it in multiple ways"? For example:

- When providing reading lists, librarians should link to more than pages in the online library catalog. They can link to open-source options when available. They should provide access to the audio versions of the book, online and in the library itself. They can do the same thing with movies related to the titles and soundtracks. They should link to reviews they've written on Amazon, to the Facebook pages and Twitter accounts of authors and to Wikipedia pages with information about the series or other works by the author.

- If the library provides physical space and staff resources for studying, groups, social events, etc., it should do so in online environments too.

- Libraries should make the online library catalog and website available on multiple platforms and tablet-and mobile-friendly.

- Librarians should let users know about alternatives to the library's offerings; such as local book stores, subject-matter experts, listservs, Facebook groups, etc. They should acknowledge the fact that users are going to be looking for resources in a variety of places and should make those overlaps known.

The more pathways librarians provide to success, the more likely that the pathways will be accessible, preferable and memorable to users.

Increase use through marketing and social networking

One of the largest barriers to library use is embodied in the age-old statement, "I had no idea that the library did that or had that!"

Librarians who work in an academic library have likely either heard a story or directly experienced a case of students purchasing personal access to resources that the library already provides. Working on a paper late at night, needing a legitimate citation, the student enters credit card information into a publisher's site and pays out of pocket for limited access, for a limited time, to one small portion of what they could have had accessed through the library website, if only they'd known to log in.

> Surprise is continually expressed when the public discover the width of [the library's] service and the catholicity of its interests. 'I didn't know that you had Music books!' 'Are you open on holidays? I didn't know that.' 'I didn't know that your catalogue is so analytic.' Such expressions as these... are a disquieting indication that a knowledge of the services he offers has not yet spread over the entire public. They make it evident that well considered publicity is as necessary for the public library as for a commercial firm."
> —Ranganathan 1931, 315–16

In most countries, advertising is seen as an appropriate and efficient way to alert audiences to information about everything from products to politics, public services and pandemics. Advertising and marketing is incredibly widespread for one very good reason: when done well, it works.

When librarians examine the return on investment for any piece of content their libraries provide, they reveal two ways to improve the value calculation: lower the price or increase the number of people who discover, access and use the material.

Hint: Librarians rarely will be able to ask for a 50% reduction in price, but they can aim to double the number of times people use the library's resources. Simple advertising campaigns need not be expensive, but they must be ongoing, because marketing research continually has shown that frequency (how often a message is seen) and recency (how recently a message has been seen) are keys to effective advertising. Doing a one-shot flyer on dorm room doors about new databases is not the answer. The answer is providing ongoing messaging in those places where your users are getting their information and engaging with others in other information-seeking behaviors.

When it comes to social networking librarians should make an effort to make their services as socially shareable as possible. Many patrons report that in the old days when there were stamp cards in the back of books, they enjoyed seeing who in the community or at school had checked out a book. That provides a social context for reading and discovery. What digital, web-based versions of that experience can libraries put into place for their users?

- Post reviews that mention users' names (with permission);
- "Share/Tweet this" buttons not just for the library website but also for materials and services;

- Participate in subject-and location-based Facebook groups that already exist, either casually or as a transparently available library consultant to the group;

- Follow and re-Tweet faculty posts related to research, resources and subjects of interest;

- Provide a weekly media digest of online mentions, news, Tweets, etc. related to a particular group or subject; and

- Keep up to date on trending topics and popular #hashtags in order to contribute related library resources and links.

Taking it a step further, Popova (2011) explains that great curators pique curiosity by engaging their patrons by explaining the modern and current relevance of an item rather than merely presenting it:

> Framing cultural importance first to magnify our motivation to engage with information. Someone who simply shares a link to a beautiful illuminated manuscript from the 13th century might grab your ephemeral attention for a fleeting moment of visual delight, but someone who shares that manuscript in the context of how it relates to today's ideals and challenges of publishing, to our shared understanding of creative labor and the changing value systems of authorship, will help integrate this archival item with your existing knowledge and interests, bridging your curiosity with your motivations to truly engage with the content. (Popova 2011)

No matter how discoverable and accessible the library's resources are, they are going to compete with many other sources for attention. Advertising not only will help promote "every book" within users' workflows but also will enhance the library's brand as an information source.

Conclusion

> " So they use New York Times continuously for like the 30 years. New York Times, it has changed. So I want to know like what years New York Times was used to gather data. I'm sure they used more than one newspaper. Also, I want to know which ones those were, for example."
> —Ph.D. Student, CBU03, Male, DIPIR, Politics and International Relations

As the quote above makes clear, sometimes "every book" doesn't even mean the book itself. It may mean the bibliography of the book, how it was used, who quoted it, how often, in what formats, how it was received or reviewed, etc. The right book may, in fact, be pieces and parts from many books, blogs, comments, videos, presentations and metadata.

The right piece of content—the exact right information that advances a user's need—always has been dependent on context, but never more so than now, when so many people are using so many powerful, new tools to discover, access and use information.

In his essay, "The Universal Library," science historian George Dyson (son of physicist Freeman Dyson and brother of technologist Esther Dyson) notes:

> The bound universe has been divided, in recent discussions over the digitization of books, into works in the public domain on one side, works under active copyright on the other, and a vast sea of inactive titles drifting in between. For those who dream of a Universal Library, however, any such classification is deficient, because it neglects the most important sector of the literary universe—books that have not been written yet. (Dyson 2014)

What Dyson is, slyly, hinting at is that we've come to the point at which the provision of information resources at unheard of scales has become somehow both incredibly useful and yet, at the same time, mundane.

- Routine Google searches turn up millions of results;

- Wikipedia hosts, as of April 2014, more than 32 million pages;

- HathiTrust provides open access to more than 11,145,244 volumes (HathiTrust 2014);

- Half of all adult Facebook users have more than 200 friends in their networks (Smith 2014); and

- LinkedIn, as of April 2014, has professional profiles for more than 277 million people, which is more than the adult population of the United States.

After awhile, we become numb to numbers in the millions and billions used to describe the Web.

We get it—it's huge, to the point where, for most of us, it might as well be infinite.

But it's not, of course. Especially in the eyes of a researcher about to add data to a study, an author promoting her work on YouTube or a community loading articles online as they try to maintain transparency about a public works program. For them, the "book" in "every book its reader" has moved from a record of something in the past to an active part of an important project with goals that start today and reach more compellingly into the future. They have moved from the "bound universe" that Dyson describes into a state he describes as "the most important sector of the library universe" (Dyson 2014).

Ranganathan says of cross-referencing in the library:

> [If] the authorities have any faith in the Third Law, they should provide for a profusion of cross-references. They should provide the necessary technical staff to have the contents of every one of the books of the library analyzed threadbare and brought to the notice of every possible class of readers by means of appropriate cross-references. (Ranganathan 1931, 312)

How is that possible, though, when "every book" no longer means "every one of the books of the library" but applies to content across all kinds of formats and media, in areas which the library has no direct control?

The answer lies in a quote we referenced earlier:

> The requirement of the Third Law defies and transcends machinery. It will always require the provision of human beings as 'canvassing agents' for books. (Ranganathan 1931, 312–13)

While the library may have no direct control, librarians can work together toward finding ways to connect people to the "10% that's not crud" from each user's point of view. This view provides both a sobering limitation on what we can expect from our technology and an encouraging vision about the future importance of library staff in an expanding information environment.

References

Anderson, Kent. 2012. Intellectual access—it takes more than accessibility. *The Scholarly Kitchen* (May 23), http://scholarlykitchen.sspnet.org/2012/05/23/intellectual-access-it-takes-more-than-accessibility/?utm_source=WhatCountsEmail&utm_medium=Above%20the%20Fold&utm_campaign=Above%20the%20Fold.

Barry, Carol L. 1994. User-defined relevance criteria: An exploratory study. *Journal of the American Society for Information Science* 45, no. 3: 149-59.

Carlson, Samuelle, and Ben Anderson. 2007. What are data? The many kinds of data and their implications for data re-use. *Journal of Computer-Mediated Communication* 12, no. 2: 635–61. Doi: 10.1111/j.1083-6101.2007.00342.

Cloonan, Michele V., and John G. Dove. 2005. Ranganathan online: Do digital libraries violate the Third Law? *Library Journal* 130, no. 6: 58-60.

Connaway, Lynn Silipigni, and Timothy J. Dickey. 2010. *The digital information seeker: Report of findings from selected OCLC, RIN, and JISC user behavior projects.* n.p.: Higher Education Funding Council for England (HEFCE). http://www.jisc.ac.uk/media/documents/publications/reports/2010/digitalinformationseekerreport.pdf.

Connaway, Lynn Silipign, Donna Lanclos, and Erin M. Hood. 2013a. "I always stick with the first thing that comes up on Google…" Where people go for information, what they use, and why. *EDUCAUSE Review Online* (December 6), http://www.educause.edu/ero/article/i-always-stick-first-thing-comes-google-where-people-go-information-what-they-use-and-why.

Connaway, Lynn Silipigni, Donna Lanclos, and Erin M. Hood. 2013b. "I find Google a lot easier than going to the library website." Imagine ways to innovate and inspire students to use the academic library. *Proceedings of the Association of College & Research Libraries (ACRL) 2013 conference, April 10-13, 2013, Indianapolis, IN.* Chicago: Association of College & Research Libraries. http://www.ala.org/acrl/sites/ala.org.acrl/files/content/conferences/confsandpreconfs/2013/papers/Connaway_Google.pdf.

Connaway, Lynn Silipigni, Chandra Prabha, and Timothy J. Dickey. 2006. *Sense-making the information confluence: The whys and hows of college and university user satisficing of information needs. Phase III: Focus group interview study.* Report on National Leadership Grant LG-02-03-0062-03, to Institute of Museum and Library Services, Washington, DC. Columbus, OH: School of Communication, The Ohio State University.

Connaway, Lynn Silipigni, Marie L. Radford, Timothy J. Dickey, Jocelyn De Angelis Williams, and Patrick Confer. 2008. Sense-making and synchronicity: Information-seeking behaviors of

Millennials and Baby Boomers. *Libri* 58, no. 2: 123-35. http://www.oclc.org/resources/research/publications/library/2008/connaway-libri.pdf.

Dempsey, Lorcan. 2008. Always on: Libraries in a world of permanent connectivity. *First Monday* 14, no. 1, http://www.firstmonday.org/htbin/cgiwrap/bin/ojs/index.php/fm/article/view/2291/207.

De Rosa, Cathy, Joanne Cantrell, Janet Hawk, and Alane Wilson. 2006. *College students' perceptions of libraries and information resources: A report to the OCLC Membership.* Dublin, OH: OCLC Online Computer Library Center.

Dervin, Brenda, CarrieLynn D. Reinhard, Zack Y. Kerr, Mei Song, and Fei C. Shen. 2006. *Sense-making the information confluence: The whys and hows of college and university User satisficing of information needs. Phase II: Sense-making online survey and phone interview study.* Report on National Leadership Grant LG-02-03-0062-03 to Institute of Museum and Library Services, Washington, DC. Columbus, OH: School of Communication, Ohio State University.

DeSantis, Nick. 2012. On Facebook, librarian brings 2 students from the early 1900s to life. *Wired Campus* (January 6), http://chronicle.com/blogs/wiredcampus/on-facebook-librarian-brings-two-students-from-the-early-1900s-to-life/34845.

Dyson, George. 2014. The universal library. *Edge* (May 28), http://edge.org/conversation/the-universal-librar.

Elder, Danielle, R. Niccole Westbrook, and Michele Reilly. 2012. Wikipedia lover, not a hater: Harnessing Wikipedia to increase the discoverability of library resources. *Journal of Web Librarianship* 6, no. 1: 32-44. DOI:10.1080/19322909.2012.641808.

Faniel, Ixchel M., and Trond E. Jacobsen. 2010. Reusing scientific data: How earthquake engineering researchers assess the reusability of colleagues' data. *Computer Supported Cooperative Work* 19, no. 3-4: 355-75.

Faniel, Ixchel, Eric Kansa, Sarah Whitcher Kansa, Julianna Barrera-Gomez, and Elizabeth Yakel. 2013. The challenges of digging data: A study of context in archaeological data reuse. In *JCDL 2013 Proceedings of the 13th ACM/IEEE-CS Joint Conference on Digital Libraries*, 295-304. New York: ACM. http://dx.doi.org/10.1145/2467696.2467712.

Faniel, Ixchel M., Adam Kriesberg, and Elizabeth Yakel. 2012. Data reuse and sensemaking among novice social scientists. Paper presented at the annual meeting of the American Society for Information Science and Technology, October 26-31, in Baltimore, MD.

Greenfield, Jeremy. 2012. Discoverability and marketing are publishing company differentiators, says perseus CMO. *DBW Digital Book World* (May 30), http://www.digitalbookworld.com/2012/discoverability-and-marketing-are-publishing-company-differentiators-says-perseus-cmo/.

HathiTrust. 2014. Statistics information. Hathi Trust Digital Library. Last accessed May 28, 2014. http://www.hathitrust.org/statistics_info.

Head, Alison J., and Michael B. Eisenberg. 2010. *How college students evaluate and use information in the digital age.* Project Information Literacy progress report. Seattle: The Information School, University of Washington.

Johnson, Stephen. 2005. *Everything bad is good for you: How today's popular culture is actually making us smarter.* New York: Riverhead Books.

Kriesberg, Adam, Rebecca D. Frank, Ixchel M. Faniel, and Elizabeth Yakel. 2013. The role of data reuse in the apprenticeship process. *ASIST 2013, November 1-6, 2013, Montreal, Quebec, Canada.*

Lally, Ann. 2009. Using Wikipedia to highlight digital collections at the University of Washington. *The Interactive Archivist* (May 18), http://interactivearchivist.archivists.org/case-studies/wikipedia-at-uw/#future.

Lally, Ann M., and Carolyn E. Dunford. 2007. Using Wikipedia to extend digital collections. *D-Lib Magazine* 13, no. 5/6, http://www.dlib.org/dlib/may07/lally/05lally.html.

Popova, Maria. 2011. Accessibility vs. access: How the rhetoric of "rare" is changing in the age of information abundance. *Nieman Journalism Lab* (August 23), http://www.niemanlab.org/2011/08/accessibility-vs-access-how-the-rhetoric-of-rare-is-changing-in-the-age-of-information-abundance/.

Prabha, Chandra, Lynn Silipigni Connaway, and Timothy J. Dickey. 2006. *Sense-making the information confluence: The whys and hows of college and university user satisficing of information needs. Phase IV: Semi-structured interview study.* Report on National Leadership Grant LG-02-03-0062-03, to Institute of Museum and Library Services, Washington, DC. Columbus, OH: School of Communication, The Ohio State University.

Radford, Marie L., and Lynn Silipigni Connaway. 2008. *Seeking synchronicity: Evaluating virtual reference services from user, non-user, and librarian perspectives: IMLS final performance report.* Report on Grant LG-06-05-0109-05, to Institute of Museum and Library Services, Washington, DC. Dublin, OH: OCLC Online Computer Library Center.

Raiders of the Lost Ark. 1981. Directed by Steven Spielberg. Hollywood: Paramount Pictures, 2008. DVD.

Ranganathan, Shiyali Ramamrita. 1931. *The five laws of library science.* London: Edward Goldston, Ltd.

Research Information Network. 2006. *Researchers and discovery services: Behaviour, perceptions and needs.* London: Research Information Network.

Rieh, Soo Young. 2002. Judgment of information quality and cognitive authority in the web. *Journal of the American Society for Information Science and Technology* 53, no. 2: 145–61. Doi:10.1002/asi.10017.

Rolland, Betsy, and Charlotte P. Lee. 2013. Beyond trust and reliability: Reusing data in collaborative cancer epidemiology research. In *Collaboration and sharing in scientific work*, 435–44. New York: ACM.

Smith, Aaron. 2014. 6 new facts about Facebook. *Fact Tank* (February 3), http://www.pewresearch.org/fact-tank/2014/02/03/6-new-facts-about-facebook/.

Spencer, Neil. 2012. How much data is created every minute? *Visual News* (June 19), http://www.visualnews.com/2012/06/19/how-much-data-created-every-minute/?view=infographic.

Szajewski, Michael. 2013. Using Wikipedia to enhance the visibility of digitized archival assets. *D-Lib Magazine* 19, no. 3/4, http://www.dlib.org/dlib/march13/szajewski/03szajewski.html.

TV Tropes contributors. Sturgeon's Law. TV Tropes. http://tvtropes.org/pmwiki/pmwiki.php/Main/SturgeonsLaw.

Wang, Peiling, and Dagobert Soergel. 1998. A cognitive model of document use during a research project. Study I. Document selection. *Journal of the American Society for Information Science* 49, no. 2: 115–33.

Wikipedia contributors. 2014. Sturgeon's Law. Wikipedia, The Free Encyclopedia. http://en.wikipedia.org/wiki/Sturgeon%27s_law.

Wong, William, Hanna Stelmaszewska, Balbir Barn, Nazlin Bhimani, and Sukhbinder Barn. 2009. *JISC user behaviour observational study: User behaviour in resource discovery. Final report.* http://www.jisc.ac.uk/publications/programmerelated/2010/ubirdfinalreport.aspx.

Yakel, Elizabeth, Ixchel Faniel, Adam Kriesberg, and Ayoung Yoon. 2013. Trust in digital repositories. *The International Journal of Digital Curation* 8, no. 1, http://www.ijdc.net/index.php/ijdc/article/view/8.1.143/303.

Zimmerman, Ann S. 2008. New knowledge from old data: The role of standards in the sharing and reuse of ecological data. *Science, Technology & Human Values* 33, no. 5: 631–52. Doi: 10.1177/0162243907306704.

5

A library is a growing organism.

> "
> It is an accepted biological fact that a growing organism alone will survive. An organism which ceases to grow will petrify and perish. The Fifth Law invites our attention to the fact that the library, as an institution, has all the attributes of a growing organism. A growing organism takes in new matter, casts off old matter, changes in size and takes new shapes and forms."
> **—Ranganathan 1931, 382**

The new fifth law: A library is a growing organism

It is true. The library is growing, but by what and whose measure? We proposed in Chapter 1 that "save the time of the reader" is now the most important of Ranganathan's laws since time, not content, is now the scarcest resource for most library users. If we apply this concept to his fifth law, "a library is a growing organism," we have to ask the question: What does it mean for libraries to grow in today's content-rich, time-poor, attention-driven environment?

Ranganathan (1931) considered books, staff and readers as major parts of the library capable of growth. He discussed these three factors together because he believed growth and change in any one of them affected the others. Although not named explicitly along with the other three, he also discussed growth in terms of the library's physical infrastructure, such as the book racks, reading rooms, catalog room and reference desk.

Ranganathan focused his discussions of growth on the size of these four factors. In the next section, we consider recent growth and change in these four factors. Then we discuss our interpretation of the law. Unlike prior chapters, our interpretation of the law does not include a rephrasing of the law itself. Instead, we propose an additional factor libraries may want to consider growing.

Examining the law in today's environment

> " Okay, so the library may not be a quiet place with an imposing reference desk and paper card catalog. Well, guess what? It's also not a closed place with books behind bars open only to the very wealthy. Nor is it an archive of papyrus rolls. But this is okay—change is a constant, and we need to learn to deal with it. No matter what type of library you're in or what you do in it, it's important to remember that you are in a service industry."
> **—Glassmeyer 2010, 24**

In addition to Glassmeyer, a variety of other researchers and writers have reflected on Ranganathan's ideas of growth and generally agree that the law is still quite useful, especially when enhanced with new examples and clarifications. We too have addressed instances of library growth and change in our discussions of laws 1–4. In the sections that follow, we highlight some of them and how they relate to the collection, staff, infrastructure and patron use.

The collection

From the perspective of the library collection, growth involves layering new, largely digital technologies into the equation, which is well described by Kwanya, Stilwell, and Underwood (2010). The authors explain that electronic materials, digitization efforts, services and new kinds of infrastructure for remote access all need to be included in any definition of growth. Take the sheer number of books, articles, databases, movies, maps, etc. provided by most libraries today. The collections dwarf what was available in the early 20th century. But when compared to the Web content that is now easily accessible, we have a situation in which the growth of library materials often looks, if not irrelevant, at least tepid. For instance, a library may make a million more items accessible, but how important is that for users with access to billions of webpages? How does the library grab their attention? How do they know what content is best for their needs—what content is relevant or credible?

> " There are no guidelines on the Web. Anyone can publish—and does. Librarians can play an important role in weeding through the dross and establishing annotated lists of links that patrons can feel confident about using."
> **—Noruzi 2004**

Noruzi (2004) suggests that providing access to content may involve a more intense and wide-ranging winnowing process on the part of librarians than traditional acquisition activities alone. This adds an important editorial element to the idea of the library collection that encompasses not just what the library owns, licenses and holds, but also what it values. The ability to do this successfully requires increased librarian training and changes to the library infrastructure.

We also have seen growth in the collection with respect to the data being generated within academic research communities. Data are a relatively new type of material entering the collection given the rise of e-research and federal funding agency mandates. However, traditional metadata, storage, reference and discovery tools simply will not work with data about data in the same way they do with data about content. We've seen that this has implications not only for the collection but also for staff, infrastructure, and patron use.

Library staff

Library budgets are being reduced or are stagnant, and in many libraries, staff costs make up almost half the costs of operating a library. The U.S. Department of Education (Phan, Hardesty, and Hug 2014, 11) reported that total salaries comprise 49.1% of academic library budgets. Similarly, total salaries comprise 67.0% of academic library budgets as reported by the Institute of Museum and Library Services (70). This means that there are limited or no available funds for creating new positions and hiring new personnel.

Within the profession, there has been more talk about libraries doing more with less and repurposing staff than about growth in staff positions. But this may not be that unusual. Dasgupta notes that librarian roles shift with users' needs and technology advances. With open access came decreased demand for counter staff and attendants and increased demand for staff in public service and acquisitions and collections (Dasgupta 2007). New kinds of media literacy are demanding new kinds of library activities, many of which have very different requirements. A survey conducted for Research Libraries UK found skill gaps in nine key areas in which subject librarians could be supporting researchers' needs; the top three were preservation of research outputs, data management and curation activities, and compliance with funding agency mandates (Auckland 2012).

Even though many librarians may want to hire new staff with these skills, a survey found that the reality for most will be training existing staff. There are a number of continuing education programs and workshops focused on skill development and community building being offered (Jahnke, Asher, and Keralis 2012). The question is whether supply is meeting demand. In a survey of library directors, 52% reassigned or were planning to reassign staff to support research data services compared to 28% who hired or were planning to hire new staff (Tenopir, Birch, and Allard 2012). The latter are likely relying on new library and information science graduates of data curation programs at major universities (Harris-Pierce and Liu 2012; Palmer et al. 2013) and the two year post-doctoral fellowship program being offered by the Council on Library and Information Resources (CLIR) (Keralis 2012).

The infrastructure

Growth of infrastructure isn't just a reflection of growth in the volume of content, but it's growth in whatever resources are necessary to meet service demands. Gorman (1998) makes the point that the use of computers within the library has demanded more of the library's space and infrastructure.

As use of the collection has shifted to electronic resources, we've seen changes in the library's physical and technical infrastructure. Librarians have had to rethink the spaces formerly occupied by print books. We've discussed cases in which space has been successfully repurposed into study areas, learning commons and makerspaces. In some cases though, institutions and communities are asking that libraries relinquish space to accommodate non-library offices and classrooms (Tobia and Feldman 2010). Regardless of how space is being repurposed, the overall sense is that, while there are many intriguing changes in the nature of library space, in general, square footage is not increasing.

While many libraries have completed renovations to repurpose space and to accommodate the changing study and work habits and behaviors of the community, there also have been new constructions of library buildings (Millar 2013; Sadler 2012). The Hunt Library at North Carolina State University, which opened in January 2013, has been referred to as "the library of the future" (Rock 2013). The library's design resulted from ongoing discussions with faculty and students. "They [the students and faculty] didn't ask for specific things—but they asked for a building that would keep changing, keep growing, and would give them a chance to change and grow with it, to keep up with technology" (Huler 2014). It demonstrates how changes in the information environment have forced librarians to rethink the role of the library and how it can become more about collaborating, learning, teaching, creating, playing, relaxing, studying and researching with the aid of physical space, people, media and technology.

Patron use

Kwanya, Stilwell, and Underwood (2010, 10) define "growth as extending beyond the simplicity of numbers and size and incorporating complexities relating to diverse user needs and wants." We've discussed this as an area in which today's librarians can focus their efforts and have a real impact. To promote the value of academic libraries, the Association of College and Research Libraries (ACRL) of the American Library Association (ALA) developed an initiative based on user-centered assessment techniques and theories (http://www.acrl.ala.org/value/). The initiative promotes accountability and evidence-based research to assess library services and programs from the users' perspectives. As an outcome-based measure, assessment focuses on "the ways in which library users are changed as a result of their contact with the library's resources and programs" (Academic Library Outcomes Assessment Task Force Committee 1998).

The objective is to apply the knowledge gained about users toward improvements in existing services as well as the creation of new services. In order to determine what collections to maintain in which formats, how to allocate and design infrastructure and what roles and responsibilities to assign staff and how to train them, it is imperative to know how people use the collections and infrastructure and where they need assistance and education from the library staff. Growth within shifting contexts means growing whatever elements of collection, staff, infrastructure and patron use that are currently part of our users' expectations. Definitions of library services will change. We need to grow the ways users can engage with whatever they value from libraries, whether papyrus rolls, makerspaces or data management instruction.

Our interpretation of the law

We agree that "a library is a growing organism." There is a need for continual evolution of the library based on the needs and behaviors of current and prospective users. We have seen this in the experiences of librarians, and we have described instances of it in our discussions of laws 1–4. We offer no reinterpretation of the law. However, we do want to expand what growth means in today's highly connected, competitive and shifting information environment. Drawing from Ranganathan's metaphor, we propose another major area of a library that is capable of growth:

> ***Share of attention.***

Share of attention boils down to a simple question: What portion of individuals' time is spent using library services and resources for getting information? Some media analysts use the term to describe the total amount of time a person has available to spend on activities and materials of choice (Blanchard 2006; Dennis 2011). So, for example, television has experienced a decline in share of attention relative to online activities such as Facebook.

We believe share of attention is essential to promoting growth and change in libraries across all the other dimensions—collection, staff, infrastructure, patron use. Toward that end, we discuss three ways to think about nurturing its growth:

- Relevance

- Visibility

- Unique capabilities

These metrics suggest a dramatic difference in how libraries need to measure growth and success. But if, as we've said, the most important of Ranganathan's laws today is "save the time of the reader," we need to find ways that factor time, convenience and usefulness into library metrics. We propose that libraries measure their relevance compared to (and in conjunction with) other information resources, seek to increase visibility within those environments, and differentiate themselves through their distinctive, expert service.

Relevance

Before trying to measure the relevance of any service, it is important to have a good idea of which products and services fall within a reasonable range of users' choices for what libraries offer. In other words, what library resources and services are used, or not used, and more importantly, why are they used or not used? Librarians also need to specify the ways their libraries are, and want to be, relevant and then ask which information resources and sites their communities use could be improved or complemented by library services. Carr (2014) suggests enabling users to select materials on demand, referred to as demand-driven acquisition (DDA), as another way to grow the library; it gives a degree of control back to the users and entices them to try library services and resources.

Librarians know how to run libraries. While being an expert on libraries is an excellent skill inside a library, most of our users are spending most of their time outside of libraries. They are searching and sharing in the online spaces that are saturating every aspect of their personal, educational and working lives. According to Dempsey (2012), in a digital, networked world where access and discovery are at Web scale, the library is just one of many information service providers and, as such, needs to consider providing an "inside-out" library experience. To be considered relevant within people's share of attention, libraries need to be discovered not only by their local community through library services but also by the larger Web population through external sites and services.

Regardless of whether a user is working within the bounds of a library-specific service to select, discover and access library materials or doing so from the outside, the emerging expectation is that the quality of service and interconnectedness of resources need to meet certain standards in order to be relevant.

Visibility

No matter how good library services are, how complete library collections or how awesome library staff, if people don't know what libraries offer, they won't use them. The perception of marketing within libraries has undergone a positive shift in the past decade, but for many libraries it still is an ancillary function. A major finding in *Perceptions of Libraries and Information Resources* is that most people do not know the library services being offered or the various formats of material available for use (De Rosa et al. 2005).

Research suggests a library's value can be demonstrated through various marketing activities, such as promotion of collections and services, advertisement of the library brand and resources and integration with external services users employ, such as Web browsers, Facebook, Twitter and Wikipedia (Connaway, Dickey, and Radford 2011). We've discussed several initiatives and studies that have been quite creative in raising the visibility of libraries and library resources when discussing laws 1—4. We provide three additional examples below.

Wikipedian in Residence Projects. Galleries, libraries, archives and museums host Wikipedians to help contribute entries to Wikipedia related to the institution's resources and services to serve as a liaison between the institution and the Wikipedia community and to perform outreach activities for staff and the general public (Outreach Wiki contributors). These kinds of projects increase visibility of institutional resources and services within individuals' routine work practices and activities.

Slam the Boards and Enquire Initiatives. With Slam the Boards, librarians participate in answer boards and social question and answer (SQA) sites to answer questions during pre-determined times. At the end of each answer, users are told that a librarian provided the information; the objective is to let users know that libraries and librarians are a viable alternative for users information needs (Kearns 2012). Enquire is a United Kingdom virtual reference service (VRS) and YahooAnswers Knowledge Partner. Put in touch with librarians offering tailored answers and personal attention, Enquire exposes library online reference services to people who would have not known about or used them otherwise (John 2011).

Building and Analyzing Online Audiences through Twitter. Yep and Shulman (2014) found that the Richard Stockton College of New Jersey's Bjork Library's Twitter account served as a gateway for information within and outside the library, which acted to raised the library's visibility. The library's Twitter followers valued access to a wider range of information that extended beyond the library, while the library extended its reach beyond its campus community (Yep and Shulman 2014).

Unique capabilities

How might librarians differentiate themselves and the library from other information service providers? What's their unique selling point (USP)? The term USP was coined by marketers and advertisers (Reeves 1961). It showcases an organization's competitive advantage which other organizations simply can't offer. In the past, an important USP for libraries was that their materials were freely and centrally available in an environment where resources were scarce and costly. While this selling point is still true, it is no longer unique (Dempsey 2008). But there are other ways libraries can and have been providing distinctive, expert services.

Libraries are unique in today's information environment in that they have, in most cases, a very strong community or institutionally-based physical presence. This sets them apart from almost all online information choices. One cannot simply walk into Amazon or call up Facebook and ask a question. Nobody from LinkedIn will sit down with you and help you design your resume. And while you can ask Google a question, there is no one available to help you phrase the question for optimal results or to help you identify the best resources to use to answer your question.

Librarians contribute an overwhelmingly positive aspect to the library brand. They are a major USP that should be promoted as the library's most valuable resource. Their ability to develop ongoing relationships in person and online should be leveraged (Connaway and Radford 2011). Their expertise is unique, valuable, and can be applied to entirely new areas of research support

(Gabridge 2009; Luce 2008; National Science Foundation 2006). Librarians have a unique role to play in supporting research processes as opposed to simply providing access to research outputs.

Seventy-two percent of researchers and librarians expect libraries to play a key role as custodians and managers of digital resources. For research data in particular, librarians have become actively involved in instructing, consulting and collaborating on data management, curation and preservation activities. More recently, the Association of Research Libraries (ARL) has partnered with the Association of American Universities (AAU) and The Association of Public and Land-grant Universities (APLU) around a SHared Access Research Ecosystem (SHARE) to ensure compliance with funding agency mandates and to meet the needs of its stakeholders (Walters and Ruttenberg 2014).

Librarians' role in developing and offering research data services is but one recent example of a USP for the library. It's not just the specific materials librarians are able to access, manage and provide over time but also their ability to apply library expertise and resources in ways that fill specific knowledge gaps.

Recommendations

In addition to the collection, staff, infrastructure and patron use, we want librarians to consider growing share of attention. In the last section, we provided three ways to nurture share of attention:

- Relevance
- Visibility
- Unique capabilities

In this section, we provide recommendations about how to measure them. Relevance, visibility and unique capabilities are not as easy to calculate as traditional metrics, such as size of catalog, number of staff, square footage, gate count and number of check outs. However, they are highly applicable to library growth within today's complex, interconnected information environment. When considering each area, keep in mind that the majority of the population does not use a library to get information; the library is not the first or main choice for most people (Connaway 2013).

Relevance

For relevance, librarians should measure the ways in which the library intersects with, resembles and complements outside services. Understanding and respecting differences and preferences provide good cues on to how to improve library services and to leverage the strengths of non-library services. Librarians should consider measuring the following:

- **Current tool use.** Librarians should identify how and why individuals use their current tools before jumping to suggest a library-based solution. According to Connaway and Radford (2011), library tools should be integrated into the services and resources people use, making these services and resources easily accessible. It is one of the best ways to provide conveniently discoverable and accessible services and resources, therefore increasing their use. Librarians need to know what users already value as part of their workflows in order to influence or try to change their choices and practices.

- **Real world use.** Librarians should make sure real world use of services is being examined, rather than how librarians use it or think their communities use it. In focus group interviews with WorldCat.org users and librarians, Connaway and Wakeling (2012) found that librarians judge library services in light of their own interaction with the tools rather than considering actual users' expectations and judgments. Librarians should make sure service improvements are being made in light of real, reported issues from users.

Visibility

For visibility, librarians should measure the ways in which users find and learn about library services. This can be done by tracking the number of clicks or views on websites and conducting brand awareness surveys and interviews. Librarians also may want to measure:

- **Connections from their most used services.** Is there a good way to get from Google, Facebook, Twitter, Wikipedia, etc. to library services? Are university departments embedding library resources and services within classes and research systems? If five professors are using lib-guides this year, what can be done to increase the number next year? If the library has 200 Facebook likes this year, it should set a goal to reach 300 next year and should try to engage with more users through the library's service options.

- **Connections to their most used services.** Since most people are not using libraries as their first or primary information source, it's important to teach them how to better use the services they prefer. If materials are provided about how to perform advanced Google searches or how to evaluate claims in Facebook discussions, users will recognize the quality of the services libraries provide and how the services improve their use of other resources.

- **Connections with other libraries.** No one library has all the answers. It is important for librarians to be cognizant of what other libraries are doing that could benefit their communities. The collective library brand improves by promoting the services and resources that other libraries make openly available.

Unique Capabilities

For libraries, unique capabilities mean those services libraries are providing that simply are not available anywhere else. Toward that end, librarians may want to consider measuring the following:

- **Cross-selling activities.** Libraries are unique among many information services in that they provide real, live people and physical and virtual spaces. This is especially important when trying to get users to embrace new library-specific services. Users don't find, use or rely on library services simply because they are available. Users are much more likely to use and recommend services to others if a trusted librarian introduces them (Connaway and Radford 2011).

- **Relationships and outcomes.** Google never knows if it provides the right link. Amazon can't tell if the book purchased for a new mother taught her something important. But a librarian has the opportunity to interact with people making it possible to provide services and sources that meet their needs and expectations. Librarians catalog books, CDs, maps, digital items, theses, articles, etc. and effectively measure their growth. How many user success stories have been cataloged in the past year? How many specific learning outcomes have been mapped?

- **Physical and virtual space.** Librarians should move beyond surveys of how library space is being used and should conduct structured observations and interviews with the people using the space. It is not enough to know that the various spaces, whether physical or virtual, are busy. Librarians need to understand when and how the spaces are being used. They run the risk of alienation if changes don't incorporate users' preferences.

- **Librarian expertise.** Librarians have a unique set of skills that can be applied to a variety of services. Yet many faculty and students can't think of librarians beyond book and journal provision. It's not enough to have the skills; librarians have to showcase them through instruction, consultation and collaboration. They have to actively think about the recurring themes presented in the questions and problems within their community, and, they have to consider how their expertise could be applied and how the value they bring matches their community's needs.

- **Being nice.** It is as important as it is obvious—being nice to people translates into positive experiences (Connaway and Radford 2011). It's especially important in terms of the library's unique ability to provide contact with real, live people capable of developing relationships face-to-face (FtF) and online. While Google can't provide positive, emotional feedback, it also can't be rude, lazy or snooty. It is important for librarians to incorporate basic customer service metrics as a growth goal.

No matter what metrics librarians pick to help determine whether or not their libraries are growing share of attention, they should make sure that the metrics reflect the perspectives of the communities being served rather than those of the librarians.

Conclusion

In some cases, measuring success in an environment where attention and time are scarce resources is like looking at golf scores: a lower number is better—fewer clicks down the wrong path and less time taken to find the right citation indicates users' ability to quickly evaluate and select relevant sources.

This is counterintuitive to the traditional idea that bigger is better and that large and growing collections, space and staff are the measure of library success. But it is not counterintuitive to how the Web works, especially in regard to search. Many commercial and entertainment websites desire stickiness. That is, they want users to stay on their site as long as possible. Growth for services like these centers around a bigger is better model—more content consumed, more ads viewed, more products bought, more brand exposure.

Google, the king of online search, provides an experience that is exactly opposite. The blank, white page with the simple search box and search results—both paid and natural—in a simple list of text links. Why? Because Google wins when users spend less time on their site. The goal is to get people to click on ads, which is how Google makes money. The less time someone spends searching on Google to find the right link, the better it is for everyone. The user gets a good result sooner. The advertiser gets a better, more qualified customer. And Google gets paid.

The "inside-out" library (Dempsey 2012) is an inversion of traditional metrics in many ways. Most content is not gathered in a centralized storage area inside the library; it is out there, and the librarians' job is to help users find it. People don't come to one location for information; they seek it as part of their information, study, work and entertainment habits, and the library's job is to engage in those places and moments with its materials and services.

In a world where Ranganathan's fourth law, "save the time of the reader," is the most important, our measurements of growth need some "inside-out" thinking too. We need to grow how we think about growth. Discussing, measuring and maintaining it needs to be a continuous process, and librarians may need to pursue challenges that are uncomfortable. A set of nice, simple, linear graphs that show how collections, staff and infrastructure grow over time relative to the size of the communities they serve is comforting. It's easy to communicate, but it's fatally flawed.

The physicist Enrico Fermi said of experimentation, "There are two possible outcomes: If the result confirms the hypothesis, then you've made a measurement. If the result is contrary to the hypothesis, then you've made a discovery" (Jevremovic 2005, 397). The process of guiding library growth needs to be one in which experimentation is not just tolerated or accepted but actively sought out and brought into planning processes and everyday work. The information environment and social networking landscape we are living in is so new, so big and changes so quickly that anything less than an experimental plan is doomed to fail, because by the time we think we understand, say, MySpace, it's all about Facebook.

If Ranganathan's fifth law, "a library is a growing organism," is to remain true, we need to work together to decide what growth means. How do we measure it in an environment where convenience is king and where being as invisible as possible within our users' information searches is a sign of success?

We've suggested librarians consider growing share of attention. Sure. There probably are other areas of growth that also should be considered, and we encourage the profession to discuss and suggest additional ones, because one thing is for sure: If we don't know how to describe our growth and success, we will not know whether, as Fermi says, our results are positive or negative, discoveries or measurements.

References

Academic Library Outcomes Assessment Task Force Committee. 1998. Task force on academic library outcomes assessment report. Association of College & Research Libraries. http://www.ala.org/acrl/publications/whitepapers/taskforceacademic.

Association of College and Research Libraries. ACRL Value of Academic Libraries: An initiative from the Association of College and Research Libraries, a division of the American Library Association. http://www.acrl.ala.org/value/.

Auckland, Mary. 2012. *Re-skilling for research*. London: Research Information Network. http://www.rluk.ac.uk/files/RLUK%20Re-skilling.pdf.

Blanchard, Olivier. 2006. The continuing shift from "market share" to "attention share." *Corante* (September 22), http://marketing.corante.com/editorial/archives/2006/09/post_5.php.

Carr, Patrick L. 2014. Reimagining the library as a technology: An analysis of Ranganathan's Five Laws of Library Science within the social construction of technology framework. *Library Quarterly* 84, no. 2: 152-64.

Connaway, Lynn Silipigni. 2013. Why the internet is more attractive than the library. *The Serials Librarian* 64, no. 1-4: 41-56.

Connaway, Lynn Silipigni, Timothy J. Dickey, and Marie L. Radford. 2011. "If it is too inconvenient I'm not going after it:" Convenience as a critical factor in information-seeking behaviors. *Library & Information Science Research* 33, no. 3: 179-90. http://www.oclc.org/content/dam/research/publications/library/2011/connaway-lisr.pdf.

Connaway, Lynn Silipigni, and Marie L. Radford. 2011. *Seeking synchronicity: Revelations and recommendations for virtual reference*. Dublin, OH: OCLC Research. http://www.oclc.org/reports/ synchronicity/full.pdf.

Connaway, Lynn Silipigni, and Simon Wakeling. 2012. *To use or not to use WorldCat.org: An international perspective from different user groups*. Unpublished report, April 26.

Dasgupta, Arjun. 2007. "Library staff" and Ranganathan's Five Laws. *IASLIC Bulletin* 52, no. 4: 195-204.

Dempsey, Lorcan. 2008. Always on: Libraries in a world of permanent connectivity. *First Monday* 14, no. 1, http://www.firstmonday.org/htbin/cgiwrap/bin/ojs/index.php/fm/article/view/2291/207.

Dempsey, Lorcan. 2012. Thirteen ways of looking at libraries, discovery, and the catalog: Scale, workflow, attention. *EDUCAUSE Review Online* (December 10), http://www.educause.edu/ero/ article/thirteen-ways-looking-libraries-discovery-and-catalog-scale-workflow-attention.

Dennis, Steven P. 2011. Share of attention. *Steve Dennis' blog: Zen and the art & science of customer-centricity* (June 9), http://stevenpdennis.com/2011/06/09/share-of-attention-2/.

De Rosa, Cathy, Joanne Cantrell, Diane Cellentani, Janet Hawk, Lillie Jenkins, and Alane Wilson. 2005. *Perceptions of libraries and information resources: A report to the OCLC Membership*. Dublin, OH: OCLC Online Computer Library Center.

Gabridge, Tracy. 2009. The last mile: Liaison roles in curating science and engineering research data. *Research Library Issues: A Bimonthly Report from ARL, CNI, and SPARC* 265: 15–21. http:// www.arl.org/bm~doc/rli-265-gabridge.pdf.

Glassmeyer, Sarah. 2010. Ranganathan 2.0. *AALL Spectrum* 14, no. 3: 22-24.

Gorman, Michael. 1998. The five laws of library science: Then & now. Excerpt of *Our singular strengths*, by Michael Gorman. School Library Journal 7: 20-23.

Harris-Pierce, Rebecca L., and Yan Quan Liu. 2012. Is data curation education at library and information science schools in North America adequate? *New Library World* 113, no. 11/12: 598–613. Doi: 10.1108/03074801211282957.

Huler, Scott. 2014. Raleigh's 50 foot librarian: Hunt Library. *Our State* (March), http://www. ourstate.com/hunt/.

Institute of Museum and Library Services. Public library revenue and expenses. Public libraries in the United States survey: Fiscal year 2011. http://www.imls.gov/assets/1/AssetManager/FY2011_ PLS_Tables_20-30A.pdf.

Jahnke, Lori, Andrew Asher, and Spencer D. C. Keralis. 2012. *The problem of data*. With an introduction by Charles Henry. Washington, DC: Council on Library and Information Resources.

Jevremovic, Tatjana. 2005. *Nuclear principles in engineering*. New York: Springer.

John, Joanne. 2011. Day or night, UK public libraries have answers. Enquire. http://enquire-uk.oclc.org/content/view/113/55/ (last modified March 3, 2014).

Kearns, Amy J. 2012. Slam the boards! Predatory reference and the online answer sites. OCLC Webjunction. http://www.webjunction.org/documents/webjunction/Slam_the_Boards_Predatory_Reference_and_the_Online_Answer_Sites.html (last modified March 21, 2012).

Keralis, Spencer D. C. 2012. Data curation education: A snapshot. In *The problem of data*, by Lori Jahnke, Andrew Asher, and Spencer D. C. Keralis, 32-39. Washington, DC: Council on Library and Information Resources.

Kwanya, Tom, Christine Stilwell, and Peter G. Underwood. 2010. Library 2.0 principles and Ranganathan's Fifth Law. *Mousaion* 28, no. 2: 1-16.

Luce, Richard E. 2008. A new value equation challenge: The emergence of eResearch and roles for research libraries. In *No brief candle: Reconceiving research libraries for the 21st century*. Washington, DC: Council on Library and Information Resources.

Millar, Erin. 2013. The university library of the future. *The Globe and Mail* (October 22), http://www.theglobeandmail.com/news/national/education/canadian-university-report/the-university-library-of-the-future/article14980161/.

National Science Foundation. 2006. *To stand the test of time: Long-term stewardship of digital datasets in science and engineering. A report to the National Science Foundation from the ARL workshop on new collaborative relationships: The role of academic libraries in the digital data universe*. Arlington, VA: National Science Foundation. http://www.arl.org/bm~doc/digdatarpt.pdf.

Noruzi, Alireza. 2004. Application of Ranganathan's Laws to the web. *Webology* 1, no. 2, http://www.webology.org/2004/v1n2/a8.html.

Outreach Wiki contributors. Wikipedian in residence. Outreach Wiki. http://outreach.wikimedia.org/w/index.php?title=Wikipedian_in_Residence&oldid=69730 (accessed June 6, 2014).

Palmer, Carole L., Nicholas M. Weber, Trevor Muñoz, and Allen H. Renear. 2013. Foundations of data curation: The pedagogy and practice of "purposeful work" with research data. *Archive Journal* 3, http://www.archivejournal.net/issue/3/archives-remixed/foundations-of-data-curation-the-pedagogy-and-practice-of-purposeful-work-with-research-data/.

Phan, Tai, Laura Hardesty, and Jamie Hug. 2014. Academic libraries: 2012. NCES 2014-038. U.S. Department of Education. Washington, DC: National Center for Education Statistics. http://nces. ed.gov/pubsearch.

Ranganathan, Shiyali Ramamrita. 1931. *The five laws of library science*. London: Edward Goldston, Ltd.

Reeves, Rosser. 1961. *Reality in advertising*. New York: Knopf.

Rock, Margaret. 2013. The future of libraries: Short on books, long on tech. *Time* (June 25), http:// techland.time.com/2013/06/25/the-future-of-libraries-short-on-books-long-on-tech/.

Sadler, Shawna. 2012. Session 3: Exploiting space as a distinctive asset. Presented at Libraries rebound: Embracing mission, maximizing impact, June 5-6, in Philadelphia, PA. https://www. youtube.com/watch?v=AmEtdVPro54&feature=youtu.be.

Tenopir, Carol, Ben Birch, and Suzie Allard. 2012. *Academic libraries and research data services: Current practices and plans for the future. An ACRL white paper*. Chicago: Association of College and Research Libraries.

Tobia, Rajia C., and Jonquil D. Feldman. 2010. Making lemonade from lemons: A case study on loss of space at the Dolph Briscoe, Jr. Library, University of Texas Health Science Center at San Antonio. *Journal of the Medical Library Association* 98, no. 1:36-39.

Walters, Tyler, and Judy Ruttenberg. 2014. Shared access research ecosystem. *EDUCAUSE Review Online* 49, no. 2: 56-57. http://www.educause.edu/ero/article/shared-access-research-ecosystem.

Yep, Jewelry, and Jason Shulman. 2014. Analyzing the library's Twitter network: Using NodeXL to visualize impact. *College & Research Library News* 75, no. 4: 177-86.

Time is
of the essence.

Conclusion

1	Embed library systems and services into users' existing workflows.
2	Know your community and its needs.
3	Develop the physical and technical infrastructure needed to deliver physical and digital materials.
4	Increase the discoverability, access and use of resources within users' existing workflows.
5	A library is a growing organism.

> " A new type of thinking is essential if mankind is to survive and move toward higher levels."
> —**Einstein 1946**

Ranganathan's *Five Laws of Library Science* has greatly influenced our thoughts on the work of libraries and librarians. Although we believe the five laws are still relevant today, our intent is to help evolve both the work done by libraries and the perceptions of libraries and librarians. In changing how we think about the five laws in terms of interpretation and order of importance (Table C1), we want to reflect the current resources and services available for use and the behaviors that people demonstrate when engaging with them. We also want to evolve our thinking and our research.

Table C1. Our interpretation and reordering of Ranganathan's five laws

Ranganathan's Original Conception	Our Interpretation and Reordering
Save the time of the reader.	Embed library systems and services into users' existing workflows.
Every person his or her book.	Know your community and its needs.
Books are for use.	Develop the physical and technical infrastructure needed to deliver physical and digital materials.
Every book its reader.	Increase the discoverability, access and use of resources within users' existing workflows.
A library is a growing organism.	

As we reflected upon the purpose and scope of the OCLC Research "User Behavior Studies & Synthesis" activity area (OCLC Research), Ranganathan's *Five Laws of Library Science* came to mind (Ranganathan 1931). This activity area centers on how users engage with technology and content. Based on our research, we suggest how libraries and librarians can better connect to those behaviors. When reviewing the literature and analyzing data from our research, we realized the five laws provide a framework for our research activity area as well as a lens through which to view the information environment.

Our intent with this publication is not to include all user behavior research. That would be virtually impossible given the significant amount of work that has been done in the area. Rather, our objective is to shape the direction of our research and put it within a context that would be timely and relevant for librarians, library researchers and information scientists as they think about making changes in practice and developing an agenda for future research.

We consider "save the time of the reader" the most important law today. It is the lack of time, not content, that is one of the most pressing issues people face. Therefore, as we set up goals for our libraries to grow and improve, we need to consider how to save users more time, in more places and in ways that are convenient and familiar to them. We have identified convenience as a primary factor in terms of choosing and getting information. Since convenience is dependent on the situation individuals find themselves in when they need information and on the context of the specific situation, it is a moving target. Individuals want it when searching for materials in the online library catalog, trying to get an answer to a specific question or sharing and revising research data.

Surprisingly, in our studies of virtual reference services (VRS), we found that many people who were asking questions through VRS actually were sitting in the library! Why did they choose VRS and not face-to-face (FtF) reference services? There are multiple reasons—not wanting to lose their seat or table, not feeling like moving or getting up from the chair, not wanting to leave personal belongings to get an answer to their questions, or not feeling comfortable asking the question FtF. Regardless of the reason, in this instance, many people saw VRS as being more convenient and faster than FtF.

There is no value in saving the time of the reader if the content needed cannot be found and accessed, which is why "every person his or her book" is next in our list. Librarians are redefining the communities they serve around e-content and a wide range of needs and demographics. Our world has been transformed by the Web, changing the way people interact with the information environment and making it necessary for librarians to change the way materials and programs are developed and delivered. One size fits none, so it is important that there are multiple options for discovery and access to resources and content based on each individual's context and situation at the time of his or her need. It requires a difficult balance between personalized and generalized service, which is why we believe it is imperative to constantly collect, analyze and discuss data to help librarians know their communities and their needs.

This transitions us to the laws "books are for use" and "every book its reader." We believe these laws are interconnected and build on each other. "Books are for use" pertains to the ongoing evaluation and assessment of the library's physical and technical infrastructure in relation to the target user's behaviors and needs. It involves looking beyond the content and its containers to the infrastructure that provides access to the content. Providing content people want depends upon the reliability and integrity of the library's systems that make it discoverable and accessible.

Our interpretation of "every book its reader" focuses on increasing the discoverability, access and use of resources and doing so within users' workflows. It is dependent on the provision of resources and systems addressed in discussions about the "books are for use" law. Interestingly, in the midst of a multitude of technically mediated delivery channels, our findings show that human sources still play a huge role in users' information activities. Librarians have an opportunity to become part of users' social networks and to put resources in the context of users' information needs.

This brings us to the final law, which underlies the previous four: "A library is a growing organism." While we do not attempt to reinterpret this law, we do discuss share of attention as another area librarians should consider growing by elevating their relevance, visibility and unique capabilities in the eyes of their users. We see share of attention as essential to the growth and change of the traditional factors—collection, staff, infrastructure and patron use.

In our research, we find library growth and change most readily apparent in library approaches to exposing content created within their institutions, from digitized special collections to research data. Not only are collections growing in size and type, but library staff is experiencing growth by retooling existing skills, hiring new people with new areas of expertise and changing users' perceptions of librarians' capabilities. The infrastructure is changing as libraries work more closely with their offices of research and information technology, researchers on their campuses, and build external relationships with other academic institutions. Patron use also is changing with increased demand for developing new kinds of literacy, new forms of engagement with librarians and new services that support their research needs.

> "
> '…would you tell me, please, which way I ought to go from here?'
> 'That depends a good deal on where you want to get to,' said the Cat.
> 'I don't much care where—' said Alice.
> 'Then it doesn't matter which way you walk,' said the Cat.
> '—so long as I get somewhere,' Alice added as an explanation.
> 'Oh, you're sure to do that,' said the Cat, 'if you only walk long enough.'"
> **—Carroll [19--?], 66**

Unlike Alice, all of us—librarians and students, teachers, researchers, scholars—have an idea of what the library is today. When asked to complete the sentence, "The library in 2020 will be _____," 24 library leaders' responses fit into the following themes: stuff, people, community, place, leadership and vision (Janes 2013). This provides a broad spectrum for librarians to build, preserve and make collections available in different formats and modes of delivery and to create both virtual and FtF services. However, in order to develop collections and services that are relevant to individuals in today's information environment, librarians must first create and develop relationships with both existing users and prospective users of these resources and programs.

With this publication, we want to consider today's information environment, how libraries and librarians are contributing to it and what can be done to enlarge their footprints. This discussion and our recommendations may seem overwhelming… and they should. We are at an apex at which there is a wealth of opportunity when it comes to the direction libraries and librarians can take. Fortunately, there is a disciplined approach to deciding what's next. A continual assessment process to measure the effectiveness of collection and service offerings can be developed. Those things that are working should be continued. There is no need for change simply for change's sake. However, when assessments indicate current offerings are not of value or interest to target groups, identifying what will meet their needs and developing, offering and monitoring the new resources and services is necessary.

Ranganathan's laws—even taken verbatim, with no changes or additions—are as helpful today as they were a century ago. They establish a framework that keeps us focused on the core values of librarianship—values that have remained remarkably consistent across a time that has seen incredible change in information technology. It is equally remarkable that the laws still are as relevant to small public libraries as they are to the largest research institutions in the world.

It should be obvious to any reader of this report that we hold Ranganathan's work and his laws in great esteem. Our intent is to reflect on them, not to supplant them. In all probability, others will continue to use his laws in this way for another hundred years, and our particular thoughts at this point in time will become helpful (hopefully) footnotes. Because, in the words of the Cheshire Cat, it helps to know "where you want to get to" as you proceed through unfamiliar or changing terrain. For us, these laws will continue to serve as a sign post.

References

Carroll, Lewis. [19--?]. *Alice's adventures in Wonderland ; and, Through the looking-glass and what Alice found there*. Illustrated by John Tenniel. New York: Hurst. http://hdl.handle.net/2027/nc01. ark:/13960/t6446qh74.

Einstein, Albert. 1946. The real problem is in the hearts of men. *The New York Times Magazine*, June 23. In an interview with Michael Amrine.

Janes, Joseph, ed. 2013. *Library 2020: Today's leading visionaries describe tomorrow's library*. Lanham, MD: Scarecrow Press.

OCLC Research. User behavior studies & synthesis. OCLC. http://oclc.org/research/activities/ubs. html.

Ranganathan, Shiyali Ramamrita. 1931. *The five laws of library science*. London: Edward Goldston, Ltd.

Bibliography

Academic Library Outcomes Assessment Task Force Committee. "Task Force on Academic Library Outcomes Assessment Report." Association of College & Research Libraries (1998), http://www.ala.org/acrl/publications/whitepapers/taskforceacademic (accessed June 1, 2014).

Aitchison, Kenneth. "Standards and Guidance in Archaeological Archiving: The Work of the Archaeological Archives Forum and the Institute for Archaeologists." *The Grey Journal* 5, no. 2 (2009): 67–71. http://www.greynet.org/images/Contents_TGJ.V5.N2.pdf.

Alves, Julio. "Unintentional Knowledge: What We Find When We're Not Looking." *The Chronicle of Higher Education: The Chronicle Review* (June 23, 2013), http://chronicle.com/article/Unintentional-Knowledge/139891/?cid=cr&utm_source=cr&utm_medium=en.

American Libraries Editors. "Manufacturing Makerspaces." *American Library Association* (February 6, 2013), http://www.americanlibrariesmagazine.org/article/manufacturing-makerspaces.

Anderson, Kent. "Intellectual Access—It Takes More Than Accessibility." *The Scholarly Kitchen* (May 23, 2012), http://scholarlykitchen.sspnet.org/2012/05/23/intellectual-access-it-takes-more-than-accessibility/?utm_source=WhatCountsEmail&utm_medium=Above%20the%20Fold&utm_campaign=Above%20the%20Fold.

Association of College and Research Libraries. "ACRL Value of Academic Libraries: An Initiative from the Association of College and Research Libraries, A Division of the American Library Association." http://www.acrl.ala.org/value/ (accessed June 1, 2014).

------. *Value of Academic Libraries: A Comprehensive Research Review and Report*. Researched by Megan Oakleaf. Chicago: Association of College and Research Libraries, 2010. http://www.acrl.ala.org/value/?page_id=21.

Auckland, Mary. *Re-skilling for Research*. London: Research Information Network, 2012. http://www.rluk.ac.uk/files/RLUK%20Re-skilling.pdf.

Barner, Keren. "The Library is a Growing Organism: Ranganathan's Fifth Law of Library Science and the Academic Library in the Digital Era." *Library Philosophy and Practice* (September 2011), http://unllib.unl.edu/LPP/barner.htm.

Barry, Carol L. "User-defined Relevance Criteria: An Exploratory Study." *Journal of the American Society for Information Science* 45, no. 3 (1994): 149-59.

Beetham, Helen, Lou McGill, and Allison Littlejohn. *Thriving in the 21st Century: Learning Literacies for the Digital Age (LLiDA Project)*. Glasgow: The Caledonian Academy, Glasgow Caledonian University, 2009. http://www.academy.gcal.ac.uk/llida/LLiDAReportJune2009.pdf.

Bhatt, R. K. "Relevance of Ranganathan's Laws of Library Science in Library Marketing." *Library Philosophy and Practice* (July 2011), http://unllib.unl.edu/LPP/bhatt.htm.

Blanchard, Olivier. "The Continuing Shift from 'Market Share' to 'Attention Share.'" *Corante* (September 22, 2006), http://marketing.corante.com/editorial/archives/2006/09/post_5.php.

Brown, Adrian, and Kathy Perrin. *A Model for the Description of Archaeological Archives*. Forth Cumberland: English Heritage Centre for Archaeology, 2000. http://www.eng-h.gov.uk/archives/archdesc.pdf.

Brown, Duncan H. *Archaeological Archives: A Guide to Best Practice in Creation, Compilation, Transfer and Curation*. n.p.: Archaeological Archives Forum, 2007. http://www.archaeologyuk.org/archives/.

Calhoun, Karen, Joanne Cantrell, Peggy Gallagher, and Janet Hawk. *Online Catalogs: What Users and Librarians Want: An OCLC Report*. Dublin, OH: OCLC, 2009.

Campbell, Eric G., Brian R. Clarridge, Manjusha Gokhale, Lauren Birenbaum, Stephen Hilgartner, Neil A. Holtzman, and David Blumenthal. "Data Withholding in Academic Genetics: Evidence from a National Survey." *JAMA: The Journal of the American Medical Association* 287, no. 4 (2002): 473-80.

Carlson, Samuelle, and Ben Anderson. "What are Data? The Many Kinds of Data and Their Implications for Data Re-use." *Journal of Computer-Mediated Communication* 12, no. 2 (2007): 635–51. Doi: 10.1111/j.1083-6101.2007.00342.

Carlson, Jacob, Michael Fosmire, C. C. Miller, and Megan Sapp Nelson. "Determining Data Information Literacy Needs: A Study of Students and Research Faculty." *portal: Libraries and the Academy* 11, no. 2 (2011): 629-57. http://muse.jhu.edu/journals/pla/summary/v011/11.2.carlson.html.

Carlson, Jake, Lisa Johnston, Brian Westra, and Mason Nichols. "Developing an Approach for Data Management Education: A Report from the Data Information Literacy Project." *The International Journal of Digital Curation* 8, no. 1 (2013): 204-217. http://www.ijdc.net/index.php/ijdc/article/view/254.

Carlson, Jake, and Marianne Stowell-Bracke. "Data Management and Sharing from the Perspective of Graduate Students: An Examination of the Culture and Practice at the Water Quality Field Station." *portal: Libraries and the Academy* 13, no. 4 (2013): 343-61.

Carr, Patrick L. "Reimagining the Library as a Technology: An Analysis of Ranganathan's Five Laws of Library Science within the Social Construction of Technology Framework." *Library Quarterly* 84, no. 2 (2014): 152-64.

Carroll, Lewis. *Alice's Adventures in Wonderland ; and, Through the Looking-glass and What Alice Found There*. Illustrated by John Tenniel. New York: Hurst, [19--?]. http://hdl.handle.net/2027/nc01.ark:/13960/t6446qh74.

Case, Donald Owen. *Looking for Information: A Survey of Research on Information Seeking, Needs and Behavior*. Bingley, UK: Emerald Group, 2012.

Centre for Information Behaviour and the Evaluation of Research. *Information Behaviour of the Researcher of the Future: A CIBER Briefing Paper*. London: CIBER, 2008.

Choudhury, G. Sayeed. "Case Study in Data Curation at John Hopkins University." *Library Trends* 57, no. 2 (2008): 211-20.

———. "Data Curation: An Ecological Perspective." *College & Research Libraries News* 71 (2010): 194-96.

Cloonan, Michele V., and John G. Dove. "Ranganathan Online: Do Digital Libraries Violate the Third Law?" *Library Journal* 130, no. 6 (2005): 58-60.

Connaway, Lynn Silipigni. "Findings from User Behavior Studies: A User's World." Presented at ALA Midwinter Meeting and Exhibits, Seattle, WA, January 28, 2013.

———. "Make Room for the Millennials." *NextSpace* 10 (2008): 18-19. http://www.oclc.org/nextspace/010/research.htm.

———. "Why the Internet is More Attractive Than the Library." *The Serials Librarian* 64, no. 1-4 (2013): 41-56.

Connaway, Lynn Silipigni, and Timothy J. Dickey. *The Digital Information Seeker: Report of Findings from Selected OCLC, RIN, and JISC User Behavior Projects*. n.p.: Higher Education Funding Council for England (HEFCE), 2010. http://www.jisc.ac.uk/media/documents/publications/reports/2010/digitalinformationseekerreport.pdf.

———. *Towards a Profile of the Researcher of Today: What Can We Learn from JISC Projects? Common Themes Identified in an Analysis of JISC Virtual Research Environment and Digital Repository Projects* (2010), http://ie-repository.jisc.ac.uk/418/2/VirtualScholar_themesFromProjects_revised.pdf.

Connaway, Lynn Silipigni, Timothy J. Dickey, and Marie L. Radford. "If it is too inconvenient I'm not going after it:" Convenience as a Critical Factor in Information-seeking Behaviors. *Library & Information Science Research* 33, no. 3 (2011): 179-90. http://www.oclc.org/content/dam/research/publications/library/2011/connaway-lisr.pdf.

Connaway, Lynn Silipigni, Donna Lanclos, and Erin M. Hood. "'I always stick with the first thing that comes up on Google…' Where People Go for Information, What They Use, and Why." *EDUCAUSE Review Online* (December 6, 2013), http://www.educause.edu/ero/article/i-always-stick-first-thing-comes-google-where-people-go-information-what-they-use-and-why.

———. "'I find Google a lot easier than going to the library website.' Imagine Ways to Innovate and Inspire Students to Use the Academic Library." *Proceedings of the Association of College & Research Libraries (ACRL) 2013 Conference, April 10-13, 2013, Indianapolis, IN*. Chicago: Association of College & Research Libraries, 2013. http://www.ala.org/acrl/sites/ala.org.acrl/files/content/conferences/confsandpreconfs/2013/papers/Connaway_Google.pdf.

Connaway, Lynn Silipigni, Donna Lanclos, David White, Alison Le Cornu, and Erin M. Hood. "User-centered Decision Making: A New Model for Developing Academic Library Services and Systems." *IFLA Journal* 39, no. 1 (2013): 30-36.

Connaway, Lynn Silipigni, Chandra Prabha, and Timothy J. Dickey. *Sense-making the Information Confluence: The Whys and Hows of College and University User Satisficing of Information Needs. Phase III: Focus Group Interview Study*. Report on National Leadership Grant LG-02-03-0062-03, to Institute of Museum and Library Services, Washington, DC. Columbus, OH: School of Communication, The Ohio State University, 2006.

Connaway, Lynn Silipigni, and Marie L. Radford. *Seeking Synchronicity: Revelations and Recommendations for Virtual Reference*. Dublin, OH: OCLC Research, 2011. http://www.oclc.org/reports/synchronicity/full.pdf.

———. "Service Sea Change: Clicking with Screenagers Through Virtual Reference." In *Sailing into the Future: Charting Our Destiny: Proceedings of the Thirteenth National Conference of the Association of College and Research Libraries, March 29-April 1, 2007, Baltimore, Maryland*, edited by Hugh A. Thompson. Chicago: Association of College and Research Libraries, 2007. http://www.oclc.org/research/publications/archive/2007/connaway-acrl.pdf.

Connaway, Lynn Silipigni, Marie L. Radford, Timothy J. Dickey, Jocelyn De Angelis Williams, and Patrick Confer. "Sense-making and Synchronicity: Information-seeking Behaviors of Millennials and Baby Boomers." *Libri* 58, no. 2 (2008): 123-35. http://www.oclc.org/resources/research/publications/library/2008/connaway-libri.pdf.

Connaway, Lynn Silipigni, and Simon Wakeling. *To Use or Not to Use WorldCat.org: An International Perspective from Different User Groups*. Unpublished report, April 26, 2012.

Connaway, Lynn Silipigni, David White, and Donna Lanclos. "Visitors and Residents: What Motivates Engagement with the Digital Information Environment?" *Proceedings of the 74th ASIS&T Annual Meeting* 48 (2011): 1-7.

Connaway, Lynn Silipigni, David White, Donna Lanclos, and Alison Le Cornu. "Visitors and Residents: What Motivates Engagement with the Digital Information Environment?" *Information Research* 18, no. 1 (2013), http://informationr.net/ir/18-1/infres181.html.

Consortium of University Research Libraries, and Research Information Network. *Researchers' Use of Academic Libraries and Their Services: A Report*. London: Research Information Network and Consortium of University Research Libraries, 2007. http://www.rin.ac.uk/our-work/using-and-accessing-informationresources/researchers-use-academic-libraries-and-their-serv.

Cragin, Melissa H., Carole L. Palmer, Jacob R. Carlson, and Michael Witt. "Data Sharing, Small Science and Institutional Repositories." *Philosophical Transactions of the Royal Society* 368, no. 1926 (2010): 4023-4038. http://rsta.royalsocietypublishing.org/content/368/1926.toc.

Daniels, Morgan, Ixchel Faniel, Kathleen Fear, and Elizabeth Yakel. "Managing Fixity and Fluidity in Data Repositories." In *iConference 2012, February 7-10, 2012, Toronto, ON, Canada*, 279-286. New York: ACM, 2012.

Dasgupta, Arjun. "'Library Staff' and Ranganathan's Five Laws." *IASLIC Bulletin* 52, no. 4 (2007): 195-204.

De Belder, Kurt. 2012. "Session 1: Directly Supporting Researchers." Presented at Libraries Rebound: Embracing Mission, Maximizing Impact, Philadelphia, PA, June 5-6, 2012. https://www.youtube.com/watch?v=R9qUoVSD7HA&feature=youtu.be.

Delserone, Leslie M. "At the Watershed: Preparing for Research Data Management and Stewardship at the University of Minnesota Libraries." *Library Trends* 57, no. 2 (2008): 202-210.

Dempsey, Lorcan. "Always On: Libraries in a World of Permanent connectivity." *First Monday* 14, no. 1 (2008), http://www.firstmonday.org/htbin/cgiwrap/bin/ojs/index.php/fm/article/view/2291/207.

———. "Thirteen Ways of Looking at Libraries, Discovery, and the Catalog: Scale, Workflow, Attention." *EDUCAUSE Review Online* (December 10, 2012), http://www.educause.edu/ero/article/thirteen-ways-looking-libraries-discovery-and-catalog-scale-workflow-attention.

Dennis, Steven P. "Share of Attention." *Steve Dennis' Blog: Zen and the Art & Science of Customer-centricity* (June 9, 2011), http://stevenpdennis.com/2011/06/09/share-of-attention-2/.

De Rosa, Cathy, Joanne Cantrell, Matthew Carlson, Peggy Gallagher, Janet Hawk, and Charlotte Sturtz. *Perceptions of Libraries, 2010: Context and Community*. Dublin, OH: OCLC Online Computer Library Center, 2010.

De Rosa, Cathy, Joanne Cantrell, Diane Cellentani, Janet Hawk, Lillie Jenkins, and Alane Wilson. *Perceptions of Libraries and Information Resources: A Report to the OCLC Membership*. Dublin, OH: OCLC Online Computer Library Center, 2005.

De Rosa, Cathy, Joanne Cantrell, Janet Hawk, and Alane Wilson. *College Students' Perceptions of Libraries and Information Resources: A Report to the OCLC Membership*. Dublin, OH: OCLC Online Computer Library Center, 2006.

Dervin, Brenda, CarrieLynn D. Reinhard, Zack Y. Kerr, Mei Song, and Fei C. Shen. *Sense-making the Information Confluence: The Whys and Hows of College and University User Satisficing of Information Needs. Phase II: Sense-making Online Survey and Phone Interview Study*. Report on National Leadership Grant LG-02-03-0062-03 to Institute of Museum and Library Services, Washington, DC. Columbus, OH: School of Communication, Ohio State University, 2006.

DeSantis, Nick. "On Facebook, Librarian Brings 2 Students from the Early 1900s to Life." *Wired Campus* (January 6, 2012), http://chronicle.com/blogs/wiredcampus/on-facebook-librarian-brings-two-students-from-the-early-1900s-to-life/34845.

Diehm, Rae-Anne, and Mandy Lupton. "Approaches to Learning Information Literacy: A Phenomenographic Study." *The Journal of Academic Librarianship* 38, no. 5 (2012): 217-25.

Dyson, George. "The Universal Library." *Edge* (May 28, 2014), http://edge.org/conversation/the-universal-librar.

EDUCAUSE Learning Initiative. "7 Things You Should Know About Makerspaces." *EDUCAUSE* (April 9, 2013), http://www.educause.edu/library/resources/7-things-you-should-know-about-makerspaces.

Einstein, Albert. "The Real Problem is in the Hearts of Men." *The New York Times Magazine*, June 23, 1946. In an interview with Michael Amrine.

Elder, Danielle, R. Niccole Westbrook, and Michele Reilly. "Wikipedia Lover, Not a Hater: Harnessing Wikipedia to Increase the Discoverability of Library Resources." *Journal of Web Librarianship* 6, no. 1 (2012): 32-44. DOI:10.1080/19322909.2012.641808.

Erway, Ricky. *Starting the Conversation: University-wide Research Data Management Policy*. Dublin, OH: OCLC Research, 2013. http://www.oclc.org/content/dam/research/publications/library/2013/2013-08.pdf.

Faniel, Ixchel M. "Infusing Consumer Data Reuse Practices into Curation and Preservation Activities." Presented at the 76th Annual Meeting of the Society of American Archivists (SAA), San Diego, CA, August 11, 2012. http://files.archivists.org/conference/sandiego2012/504-Faniel.pdf.

Faniel, Ixchel M. *Unrealized Potential: The Socio-technical Challenges of a Large Scale Cyberinfrastructure Initiative*. Arlington, VA: National Science Foundation, 2009. http://hdl.handle.net/2027.42/61845.

Faniel, Ixchel, Lynn Silipigni Connaway, and Kendra Parson. "20th Annual Reference Research Forum." Presented at ALA Annual Conference & Exhibition, Las Vegas, NV, June 26-July 1, 2014.

Faniel, Ixchel M., and Trond E. Jacobsen. "Reusing Scientific Data: How Earthquake Engineering Researchers Assess the Reusability of Colleagues' Data." *Computer Supported Cooperative Work* 19, no. 3-4 (2010): 355-75.

Faniel, Ixchel, Eric Kansa, Sarah Whitcher Kansa, Julianna Barrera-Gomez, and Elizabeth Yakel. "The Challenges of Digging Data: A Study of Context in Archaeological Data Reuse." In *JCDL 2013 Proceedings of the 13th ACM/IEEE-CS Joint Conference on Digital Libraries*, 295-304. New York: ACM, 2013. http://dx.doi.org/10.1145/2467696.2467712.

Faniel, Ixchel M., Adam Kriesberg, and Elizabeth Yakel. "Data Reuse and Sensemaking Among Novice Social Scientists." Paper presented at the annual meeting of the American Society for Information Science and Technology, Baltimore, MD, October 26-31, 2012.

Faniel, Ixchel M., and Elizabeth Yakel. "Significant Properties as Contextual Metadata." *Journal of Library Metadata* 11 (2011): 155-65.

Faniel, Ixchel M., and Ann Zimmerman. "Beyond the Data Deluge: A Research Agenda for Large-scale Data Sharing and Reuse." *International Journal of Digital Curation* 6, no. 1 (2011): 58-69. http://www.ijdc.net/index.php/ijdc/article/view/163.

Fast, Karl V., and D. Grant Campbell. "'I still like Google:' University Student Perceptions of Searching OPACs and the Web." *Proceedings of the ASIS&T Annual Meeting* 41 (2004): 138-46.

Fisher, Erin. "Makerspaces Move into Academic Libraries." *ACRL TechConnect* (November 28, 2012), http://acrl.ala.org/techconnect/?p=2340.

Gabridge, Tracy. "The Last Mile: Liaison Roles in Curating Science and Engineering Research Data." *Research Library Issues: A Bimonthly Report from ARL, CNI, and SPARC* 265 (2009): 15–21. http://www.arl.org/bm~doc/rli-265-gabridge.pdf.

Glassmeyer, Sarah. "Ranganathan 2.0." *AALL Spectrum* 14, no. 3 (2010): 22-24.

Goldup, Stacey Jeanette. *Public Libraries in the Digital Age: Investing the Implementation of Ranganathan's Five Laws of Library Science in Physical and Online Library Services*. Report submitted to the School of Information Management, Victoria University of Wellington, February 2010.

Gorman, Michael. "Five New Laws of Librarianship." *American Libraries* 26, no. 8 (1995): 784-85.

———. "The Five Laws of Library Science: Then & Now." Excerpt of *Our Singular Strengths*, by Michael Gorman. *School Library Journal* 7 (1998): 20-23.

Greenfield, Jeremy. "Discoverability and Marketing are Publishing Company Differentiators, Says Perseus CMO." *DBW Digital Book World* (May 30, 2012), http://www.digitalbookworld.com/2012/ discoverability-and-marketing-are-publishing-company-differentiators-says-perseus-cmo/.

Griffiths, Aaron. "The Publication of Research Data: Researcher Attitudes and Behavior." *The International Journal of Digital Curation* 4, no. 1 (2008): 46-56. http://www.ijdc.net/index.php/ ijdc/issue/view/7.

Griffiths, José M., and Donald W. King. *InterConnections: The IMLS National Study on the Use of Libraries, Museums and the Internet: General Information Report*. Washington, DC: Institute of Museum and Library Services, 2008.

Harris-Pierce, Rebecca L., and Yan Quan Liu. "Is Data Curation Education at Library and Information Science Schools in North America Adequate?" *New Library World* 113, no. 11/12 (2012): 598–613. Doi: 10.1108/03074801211282957.

HathiTrust. "Statistics Information." Hathi Trust Digital Library. http://www.hathitrust.org/ statistics_info (accessed May 28, 2014).

Head, Alison J., and Michael B. Eisenberg. *How College Students Evaluate and Use Information in the Digital Age. Project Information Literacy Progress Report*. Seattle: The Information School, University of Washington, 2010.

———. "Lessons Learned: How College Students Seek Information in the Digital Age." Project Information Literacy Progress Report, The Information School, University of Washington (2009), http://projectinfolit.org/images/pdfs/pil_fall2009_finalv_yr1_12_2009v2.pdf.

Hey, Tony, and Anne Trefethen. "The Data Deluge: An e-Science Perspective." In *Grid Computing: Making the Global Information Infrastructure a Reality*, edited by Fran Berman, Geoffrey Fox, and Tony Hey, 809-824. Chichester, UK: Wiley, 2003.

Hiebert, Jean, and Shelly Theriault. "BLASTing the Zombies! Creative Ideas to Fight Finals Fatigue." *College & Research Libraries News* 73, no. 9 (2012): 540-69.

Holdren, John P. "Memorandum for the Heads of Executive Departments and Agencies." Washington, DC: Office of Science and Technology Policy, 2013. http://www.whitehouse.gov/sites/ default/files/microsites/ostp/ostp_public_access_memo_2013.pdf.

Huler, Scott. "Raleigh's 50 Foot Librarian: Hunt Library." *Our State* (March 2014), http://www.ourstate.com/hunt/.

Idaho Commission for Libraries. *Perceptions of Idaho's Digital Natives on Public Libraries: Statewide Focus Group Findings*. Washington, DC: Institute of Museum and Library Services, 2007.

Institute for Archaeologists. *Standard and Guidance for the Creation, Compilation, Transfer and Deposition of Archaeological Archives*. n.p.: Institute for Archaeologists, 2009. http://www.archaeologists.net/sites/default/files/node-files/Archives2009.pdf.

Institute of Museum and Library Services. "Public Library Revenue and Expenses." Public Libraries in the United States Survey: Fiscal Year 2011. http://www.imls.gov/assets/1/AssetManager/FY2011_PLS_Tables_20-30A.pdf.

Jahnke, Lori, Andrew Asher, and Spencer D. C. Keralis. *The Problem of Data*. With an introduction by Charles Henry. Washington, DC: Council on Library and Information Resources, 2012.

Janes, Joseph. *Library 2020: Today's Leading Visionaries Describe Tomorrow's Library*. Lanham, MD: Scarecrow Press, 2013.

Jevremovic, Tatjana. *Nuclear Principles in Engineering*. New York: Springer, 2005.

Jisc. "Make Your Digital Resources Easier to Discover." Quickguide (March 7, 2014). http://www.jisc.ac.uk/guides/make-your-digital-resources-easier-to-discover.

John, Joanne. "Day or Night, UK Public Libraries Have Answers." Enquire (January 25, 2011). http://enquire-uk.oclc.org/content/view/113/55/.

Johnson, Stephen. *Everything Bad Is Good For You: How Today's Popular Culture Is Actually Making Us Smarter*. New York: Riverhead Books, 2005.

Johnston, Lisa, and Cody Hanson. "e-Science at the University of Minnesota: A Collaborative Approach." *International Association of Scientific and Technological University Libraries, 31st Annual Conference* (June 22, 2010), http://docs.lib.purdue.edu/iatul2010/conf/day2/3.

Johnston, Lisa, and Jon Jeffryes. "Data Management Skills Needed by Structural Engineering Students: Case Study at the University of Minnesota." *Journal of Professional Issues in Engineering Education and Practice* 140, no. 2 (2013), http://dx.doi.org/10.1061/(ASCE)EI.1943-5541.0000154.

Kearns, Amy J. "Slam the Boards!" Predatory Reference and the Online Answer Sites. OCLC Webjunction (2012). http://www.webjunction.org/documents/webjunction/Slam_the_Boards_Predatory_Reference_and_the_Online_Answer_Sites.html.

Keralis, Spencer D. C. "Data Curation Education: A Snapshot." In *The Problem of Data*, by Lori Jahnke, Andrew Asher, and Spencer D. C. Keralis, 32-39. Washington, DC: Council on Library and Information Resources, 2012.

Kriesberg, Adam, Rebecca D. Frank, Ixchel M. Faniel, and Elizabeth Yakel. "The Role of Data Reuse in the Apprenticeship Process." *ASIST 2013, November 1-6, 2013, Montreal, Quebec, Canada* (2013).

Kwanya, Tom, Christine Stilwell, and Peter G. Underwood. "Library 2.0 Principles and Ranganathan's Fifth Law." *Mousaion* 28, no. 2 (2010): 1-16.

Lage, Kathryn, Barbara Losoff, and Jack Maness. "Receptivity to Library Involvement in Scientific Data Curation: A Case Study at the University of Colorado Boulder." *portal: Libraries and the Academy* 11, no. 4 (2011): 915-37.

Lally, Ann. "Using Wikipedia to Highlight Digital Collections at the University of Washington." *The Interactive Archivist* (May 18, 2009), http://interactivearchivist.archivists.org/case-studies/wikipedia-at-uw/#future.

Lally, Ann M., and Carolyn E. Dunford. "Using Wikipedia to Extend Digital Collections." *D-Lib Magazine* 13, no. 5/6 (2007), http://www.dlib.org/dlib/may07/lally/05lally.html.

Lankes, R. David, blog. "The Atlas of New Librarianship." http://www.newlibrarianship.org/wordpress/.

Lavoie, Brian, Eric Childress, Ricky Erway, Ixchel Faniel, Constance Malpas, Jennifer Schaffner, and Titia van der Werf. *The Evolving Scholarly Record*. Dublin, OH: OCLC Research, 2014. http://www.oclc.org/research/publications/library/2014/oclcresearch-evolving-scholarly-record-2014.pdf.

Lewicki, Roy J., and Barbara Benedict Bunker. "Developing and Maintaining Trust in Work Relationships." In *Trust in Organizations: Frontiers of Theory and Research*, edited by Roderick Kramer and Tom Tyler, 114-39. Thousand Oaks, CA: Sage Publications, 1996.

Lippincott, Joan K. "A Mobile Future for Academic Libraries." *Reference Services Review* 38, no. 2 (2010): 205-213.

Lippincott, Joan K., and Kim Duckett. "Library Space Assessment: Focusing on Learning." *Research Library Issues: A Report from ARL, CNI, and SPARC* 284 (2013): 12-21. http://publications.arl.org/rli284/.

Luce, Richard E. "A New Value Equation Challenge: The Emergence of eResearch and Roles for Research Libraries." In *No Brief Candle: Reconceiving Research Libraries for the 21st Century*. Washington, DC: Council on Library and Information Resources, 2008.

Merriam-Webster.com. "Convenience." http://www.merriam-webster.com/dictionary/convenience (accessed December 12, 2013).

Millar, Erin. "The University Library of the Future." *The Globe and Mail* (October 22, 2013), http://www.theglobeandmail.com/news/national/education/canadian-university-report/the-university-library-of-the-future/article14980161/.

National Science Foundation. *To Stand the Test of Time: Long-term Stewardship of Digital Datasets in Science and Engineering. A Report to the National Science Foundation from the ARL Workshop on New Collaborative Relationships: The Role of Academic Libraries in the Digital Data Universe.* Arlington, VA: National Science Foundation, 2006. http://www.arl.org/bm~doc/digdatarpt.pdf.

Nelson, Bryn. "Data Sharing: Empty Archives." *Nature* 461, no. 7261 (2009): 160–63. http://www.nature.com/news/2009/090909/pdf/461160a.pdf.

Newton, Mark P., C. C. Miller, and Marianne S. Bracke. "Librarian Roles in Institutional Repository Data Set Collecting: Outcomes of a Research Library Task Force." *Collection Management* 36, no. 1 (2010): 53-67. Doi: 10.1080/01462679.2011.530546.

Noruzi, Alireza. "Application of Ranganathan's Laws to the Web." *Webology* 1, no. 2 (2004), http://www.webology.org/2004/v1n2/a8.html.

Oblinger, Diana G., and James L. Oblinger, eds. *Educating the Net Generation*. Boulder: EDUCAUSE, 2005. http://www.educause.edu/content.asp?PAGE_ID=5989&bhcp=1.

OCLC Research. "User Behavior Studies & Synthesis." OCLC. http://oclc.org/research/activities/ubs.html.

Odum Library. "Odum Library Makerspace." Valdosta State University. https://www.valdosta.edu/academics/library/depts/circulation/makerspace.php.

Outreach Wiki Contributors. "Wikipedian in Residence." Outreach Wiki. http://outreach.wikimedia.org/w/index.php?title=Wikipedian_in_Residence&oldid=69730 (accessed June 6, 2014).

Palmer, Carole L., Nicholas M. Weber, Trevor Muñoz, and Allen H. Renear. "Foundations of Data Curation: The Pedagogy and Practice of 'Purposeful Work' with Research Data." *Archive Journal* 3 (2013), http://www.archivejournal.net/issue/3/archives-remixed/foundations-of-data-curation-the-pedagogy-and-practice-of-purposeful-work-with-research-data/.

Parks Canada. *Archaeological Recording Manual: Excavations and Surveys*. n.p.: Parks Canada, 2005. http://www.pc.gc.ca/eng/docs/pc/guide/fp-es/titre-title.aspx.

Partridge, Helen, and Gillian Hallam. "Educating the Millennial Generation for Evidence Based Information Practice." *Library Hi Tech* 24, no. 3 (2006): 400-419. http://www.emeraldinsight.com/journals.htm?articleid=1571818&.

Peters, Christie, and Anita Riley Dryden. "Assessing the Academic Library's Role in Campus-wide Research Data Management: A First Step at the University of Houston." *Science & Technology Libraries* 30, no. 4 (2011): 387-403. http://www.tandfonline.com/doi/pdf/10.1080/019426 2X.2011.626340.

Phan, Tai, Laura Hardesty, and Jamie Hug. *Academic Libraries: 2012*. NCES 2014-038. U.S. Department of Education. Washington, DC: National Center for Education Statistics, 2014. http://nces.ed.gov/pubsearch.

Pierard, Cindy, and Norice Lee. "Studying Space: Improving Space Planning with User Studies." *Journal of Access Services* 8 (2011): 190-207. Doi: 10.1080/15367967.2011.602258.

Pirson, Michael, and Deepak Malhotra. "Foundations of Organizational Trust: What Matters to Different Stakeholders?" *Organization Science* 22, no. 4 (2011): 1087-1104. http://pubsonline.informs.org/doi/abs/10.1287/orsc.1100.0581.

Popova, Maria. "Accessibility vs. Access: How the Rhetoric of 'Rare' is Changing in the Age of Information Abundance." *Nieman Journalism Lab* (August 23, 2011), http://www.niemanlab.org/2011/08/accessibility-vs-access-how-the-rhetoric-of-rare-is-changing-in-the-age-of-information-abundance/.

Prabha, Chandra, Lynn Silipigni Connaway, and Timothy J. Dickey. *Sense-making the Information Confluence: The Whys and Hows of College and University User Satisficing of Information Needs. Phase IV: Semi-structured Interview Study*. Report on National Leadership Grant LG-02-03-0062-03, to Institute of Museum and Library Services, Washington, DC. Columbus, OH: School of Communication, The Ohio State University, 2006.

Prieto, Adolfo G. "From Conceptual to Perceptual Reality: Trust in Digital Repositories." *Library Review* 58, no. 8 (2009): 593-606. http://www.emeraldinsight.com/journals.htm?issn=0024-2535.

Pritchard, Sarah M. "Deconstructing the Library: Reconceptualizing Collections, Spaces and Services." *Journal of Administration* 48, no. 2 (2008): 219-33. http://www.tandfonline.com/doi/abs/10.1080/01930820802231492#.U3OLI_ldVMg.

Pullinger, David. "Academics and the New Information Environment: The Impact of Local Factors on Use of Electronic Journals." *Journal of Information Science* 25, no. 2 (1999): 164-72.

Purcell, Kristen, Lee Rainie, Alan Heaps, Judy Buchanan, Linda Friedrich, Amanda Jacklin, Clara Chen, and Kathryn Zickuhr. *How Teens Do Research in the Digital World*. Washington, DC: PEW Internet & American Life Project, 2012. http://pewinternet.org/Reports/2012/Student-Research.aspx.

Radford, Marie L., and Lynn Silipigni Connaway. *Seeking Synchronicity: Evaluating Virtual Reference Services from User, Non-user, and Librarian Perspectives: IMLS Final Performance Report*. Report on Grant LG-06-05-0109-05, to Institute of Museum and Library Services, Washington, DC. Dublin, OH: OCLC Online Computer Library Center, 2008.

Raiders of the Lost Ark. Directed by Steven Spielberg. 1981. Hollywood: Paramount Pictures, 2008. DVD.

Ranganathan, Shiyali Ramamrita. *The Five Laws of Library Science*. London: Edward Goldston, Ltd, 1931.

Reeves, Rosser. *Reality in Advertising*. New York: Knopf, 1961.

Research Information Network. *Researchers and Discovery Services: Behaviour, Perceptions and Needs*. London: Research Information Network, 2006.

———. *To Share or Not to Share: Publication and Quality Assurance of Research Data Outputs*. London: Research Information Network, 2008.

Rieh, Soo Young. "Judgment of Information Quality and Cognitive Authority in the Web." *Journal of the American Society for Information Science and Technology* 53, no. 2 (2002): 145–61. Doi:10.1002/asi.10017.

Rock, Margaret. "The Future of Libraries: Short on Books, Long on Tech." *Time* (June 25, 2013), http://techland.time.com/2013/06/25/the-future-of-libraries-short-on-books-long-on-tech/.

Rolland, Betsy, and Charlotte P. Lee. "Beyond Trust and Reliability: Reusing Data in Collaborative Cancer Epidemiology Research." In *Collaboration and Sharing in Scientific Work*, 435–44. New York: ACM, 2013.

Ross, Seamus, and Andrew McHugh. "The Role of Evidence in Establishing Trust in Repositories." *D-Lib Magazine* 12, no. 7/8 (2006), http://www.dlib.org/dlib/july06/ross/07ross.html.

Rubin, Richard E. 2004. *Foundations of Library and Information Science*. New York: Neal-Schuman Publishers, 2004.

Rushkoff, Douglas. *Playing the Future: How Kids' Culture Can Teach Us to Thrive in An Age of Chaos*. New York: HarperCollins, 1996.

Sadler, Shawna. "Session 3: Exploiting Space as a Distinctive Asset." Presented at Libraries Rebound: Embracing Mission, Maximizing Impact, Philadelphia, PA, June 5-6, 2012. https://www.youtube.com/watch?v=AmEtdVPro54&feature=youtu.be.

Salo, Dorothea. "Innkeeper at the Roach Motel." *Library Trends* 57, no. 2 (2008): 98-123.

Savolainen, Reijo. "The Sense-making Theory: Reviewing the Interests of a User-centered Approach to Information Seeking and Use." *Information Processing & Management* 29, no. 1 (1993): 13-28.

Sayogo, Djoko Sigit, and Theresa A. Pardo. "Exploring the Motive for Data Publication in Open Data Initiative: Linking Intention to Action." *2012 45th Hawaii International Conference on System Sciences* (2012).

Scaramozzino, Jeanine Marie, Marisa L. Ramirez, and Karen J. McGaughey. "A Study of Faculty Data Curation Behaviors and Attitudes at a Teaching-centered University." *College & Research Libraries* 73, no. 4 (2012): 349-65. http://crl.acrl.org/content/73/4/349.full.pdf+html.

Simon, Herbert A. "A Behavioral Model of Rational Choice." In *Models of Man: Social and Rational*. New York: John Wiley & Sons, 1957.

Sitkin, Sim B., and Nancy L. Roth. "Explaining the Limited Effectiveness of Legalistic 'Remedies' for Trust/Distrust." *Organizational Science* 4 (1993): 367–92. http://www.jstor.org/stable/2634950.

Smith, Aaron. "6 New Facts About Facebook." *Fact Tank* (February 3, 2014), http://www.pewresearch.org/fact-tank/2014/02/03/6-new-facts-about-facebook/.

Soehner, Catherine, Catherine Steeves, and Jennifer Ward. *e-Science and Data Support Services: A Study of ARL Member Institutions* (2010), http://www.arl.org/bm~doc/escience_report2010.pdf.

Spencer, Neil. "How Much Data is Created Every Minute?" *Visual News* (June 19, 2012), http://www.visualnews.com/2012/06/19/how-much-data-created-every-minute/?view=infographic.

Sweeney, Richard. *Millennial Behaviors & Demographics*, http://certi.mst.edu/media/administrative/certi/documents/Article-Millennial-Behaviors.pdf (last revised December 22, 2006).

Szajewski, Michael. "Using Wikipedia to Enhance the Visibility of Digitized Archival Assets." *D-Lib Magazine* 19, no. 3/4 (2013), http://www.dlib.org/dlib/march13/szajewski/03szajewski.html.

Talja, Sanna, Heidi Keso, and Tarja Pietilainen. "The Production of 'Context' in Information Seeking Research: A Metatheoretical View." *Information Processing & Management* 35, no. 6 (1999): 751-63.

Tenopir, Carol, Suzie Allard, Kimberly Douglass, Arsev Umur Aydinoglu, Lei Wu, Eleanor Read, Maribeth Manoff, and Mike Frame. "Data Sharing by Scientists: Practices and Perceptions." *PLoS ONE* 6, no. 6 (2011): e21101. http://www.plosone.org/article/info%3Adoi%2F10.1371%2Fjournal.pone.0021101.

Tenopir, Carol, Ben Birch, and Suzie Allard. *Academic Libraries and Research Data Services: Current Practices and Plans for the Future. An ACRL White Paper*. Chicago: Association of College and Research Libraries, 2012.

Tobia, Rajia C., and Jonquil D. Feldman. "Making Lemonade from Lemons: A Case Study on Loss of Space at the Dolph Briscoe, Jr. Library, University of Texas Health Science Center at San Antonio." *Journal of the Medical Library Association* 98, no. 1 (2010): 36-39.

TV Tropes contributors. "Sturgeon's Law." TV Tropes. http://tvtropes.org/pmwiki/pmwiki.php/Main/SturgeonsLaw (accessed June 1, 2014).

Van House, Nancy. "Digital Libraries and Practices of Trust: Networked Biodiversity Information." *Social Epistemology: A Journal of Knowledge, Culture and Policy* 16, no. 1 (2002): 99. Doi: 10.1080/02691720210132833.

Van House, Nancy A., Mark H. Butler, and Lisa R. Schiff. "Cooperative Knowledge Work and Practices of Trust: Sharing Environmental Planning Data Sets." In *Proceedings of the 1998 ACM Conference On Computer Supported Cooperative Work*, 335–43. Seattle, WA: ACM, 1998. Doi:10.1145/289444.289508.

Van Scoyoc, Anna M., and Caroline Cason. "The Electronic Academic Library: Undergraduate Research Behavior in a Library Without Books." *portal: Libraries and the Academy* 6, no. 1 (2006): 47-58.

Walter, Scott. "Ranganathan Redux: The 'Five Laws' and the Future of College & Research Libraries." *College & Research Libraries* 73, no. 3 (2012): 213-15.

Walter, Virginia A., and Cindy Mediavilla. "Teens are from Neptune, Librarians are from Pluto: An Analysis of Online Reference Transactions." *Library Trends* 54, no. 2 (2005): 209–227.

Walters, Tyler, and Judy Ruttenberg. "Shared Access Research Ecosystem." *EDUCAUSE Review Online* 49, no. 2 (2014): 56-57. http://www.educause.edu/ero/article/shared-access-research-ecosystem.

Wang, Peiling, and Dagobert Soergel. "A Cognitive Model of Document Use During a Research Project. Study I. Document Selection." *Journal of the American Society for Information Science* 49, no. 2 (1998): 115–33.

Warwick, Claire, Isabel Galina, Melissa Terras, Paul Huntington, and Nikoleta Pappa. "The Master Builders: LAIRAH Research on Good Practice in the Construction of Digital Humanities Projects." *Literary and Linguistic Computing* 23, no. 3 (2008): 383-96. http://discovery.ucl.ac.uk/13810/.

Watters, Audrey. "The Case for Campus Makerspace." *Hack Education* (February 6, 2013), http://hackeducation.com/2013/02/06/the-case-for-a-campus-makerspace/.

White, David. "The Learning Black Market." *TALL Blog* (September 30, 2011), http://tallblog.conted.ox.ac.uk/index.php/2011/09/30/the-learning-black-market/.

White, David, Lynn Silipigni Connaway, Donna Lanclos, Alison Le Cornu, and Erin Hood. *Digital Visitors and Residents: Progress Report*. Report submitted to Jisc, June 2012. http://www.jisc.ac.uk/media/documents/projects/visitorsandresidentsinterim%20report.pdf.

Wikipedia contributors. "Sturgeon's Law." Wikipedia, The Free Encyclopedia. http://en.wikipedia.org/wiki/Sturgeon%27s_law (accessed June 1, 2014).

Williams, Lesley. "Making 'e' Visible." *Library Journal* 13, no. 11 (2006): 40-43.

Witt, Michael. "Institutional Repositories and Research Data Curation in a Distributed Environment." *Library Trends* 57, no. 2 (2008): 191-201.

Witt, Michael, Jacob Carlson, D. Scott Brandt, and Melissa Cragin. "Constructing Data Curation Profiles." *The International Journal of Digital Curation* 4, no. 3 (2009): 93-103.

Wong, William, Hanna Stelmaszewska, Balbir Barn, Nazlin Bhimani, and Sukhbinder Barn. *JISC User Behaviour Observational Study: User Behaviour in Resource Discovery. Final Report* (2009), http://www.jisc.ac.uk/publications/programmerelated/2010/ubirdfinalreport.aspx.

Yakel, Elizabeth, Ixchel Faniel, Eric Kansa, and Sara Kansa. "Archaeological Data: Curation, Preservation, and Reuse." Presented at the Society for American Archaeology (SAA) 78th Annual Meeting, Honolulu, HI, April 3-7, 2013. http://www.slideshare.net/oclcr/digital-archaeological-data-curation-preservation-and-reuse.

Yakel, Elizabeth, Ixchel Faniel, Adam Kriesberg, and Ayoung Yoon. "Trust in Digital Repositories." *The International Journal of Digital Curation* 8, no. 1 (2013), http://www.ijdc.net/index.php/ijdc/article/view/8.1.143/303.

Yep, Jewelry, and Jason Shulman. "Analyzing the Library's Twitter Network: Using NodeXL to Visualize Impact." *College & Research Library News* 75, no. 4 (2014): 177-86.

Yoon, Ayoung. "End Users' Trust in Data Repositories: Definition and Influences on Trust Development." *Archival Science* 14, no. 1 (2013): 17-34. Doi: 10.1007/s10502-013-9207-8.

Zickuhr, Kathryn, Lee Rainie, and Kristen Purcell. *Library Services in the Digital Age*. Washington, DC: Pew Research Center's Internet & American Life Project, 2013. http://libraries.pewinternet.org/files/legacy-pdf/PIP_Library%20services_Report.pdf.

Zimmerman, Ann S. "New Knowledge from Old Data: The Role of Standards in the Sharing and Reuse of Ecological Data." *Science, Technology & Human Values* 33, no. 5 (2008): 631–52. Doi: 10.1177/0162243907306704.